ON THE JOB TRAINING

TWYLA RIGHTER

On The Job Training
Twyla Righter

Print Edition
Copyright © 2018 by Twyla Righter

City Lights Press
An Imprint of Wolfpack Publishing
6032 Wheat Penny Avenue
Las Vegas, NV 89122

All rights reserved. No part of this book may be reproduced by any means without the prior written consent of the publisher, other than brief quotes for reviews.

Paperback ISBN 978-1-64119-573-7

Library of Congress Control Number: 2018964381

ON THE JOB TRAINING

YOUTUBE VIDEOS ARE DANGEROUS

YOUTUBE VIDEOS ARE DANGEROUS. I MEAN... REALLY... you could die. I did. (Well, not totally.) But I could have, which is almost the same thing. You doubt me I'm sure, but I am being sincere. A YouTube video nearly killed me.

I need to clarify that the YouTube video in question involved a hippie girl from somewhere in Hawaii. You should always be suspicious of Hippie girls and suspicious of Hawaii. (Get some consonants!)

But, hippie girls will always make for trouble. This is because hippies say things like, 'follow your heart, make love not war, meat is murder.' These ideas are dangerous. But, this particular hippie was not advising me to seek my balance in the way of the universe. No, she was checking out her bees. And, I too needed to check out my bees. (I own bees.)

So, hippie girl was checking out her bees, (Yes, I'm sure she was a hippie. She had dreadlocks and a tank top with no bra.) Highly shocking and inappropriate! (I'm sure you could find it if you hunted around YouTube long enough.)

So she was checking out her hives. No suite, no smoke, no veil or gloves!!!

"What the hay!" I said. "She seems to have no stings at all! And here I am with two hives of bees that start freaking out whenever we get within ten yards of their hives! Why am I so unbalanced? Why am I so un-Zen?" She mentioned how calm and gentle bees are if you just move slowly and have good energy.

Well, that was it.

I was done being the uptight bourgeois westerner. I could be Zen! I could be balanced! I bet for a few easy payments of 19.99 I could get Zen delivered to my door via Amazon Prime! But, being a bit western still, I was too impatient to wait for delivery.

I had a stern talk with myself. 'The braless Hawaiian hippie is right. You can be balanced and calm, and your bees with recognize your energy and respond! Stop the histrionics drama queen! They're just little honey bees. You got this!'

I did not got this.

This is where I died... almost.

Full of my Zen balance (but with my bra on because... come-on) I walked gently and to the hive. I got right up next to it and breathed slow, chill, energy breaths. And would you believe those bees didn't sting me? This was great! Progress. No drama. Obviously, my 5 minutes of YouTube was well spent. I am ready to join the Tibetan Masters.

Nothing like American Exceptionalism to teach you some good shortcuts for the road to enlightenment.

I now need to move the hive box with the feeder. No big thing. Lift one box off the top, set it down and then replace the lid. Maybe two minutes max.

I lift the box. Bees come pouring out of their home, not

psyched that someone is pulling it apart. I reach out with my chill energy.

My energy radiates, "Hello sisters, I am no threat, I am making a minor adjustment to your home. Be chill my sisters."

My sisters are jerks!

My sister bees are not Zen. They are not Zen at all!

They are the Attila the Hun! My face is swarmed with buzzing, bitter, bee women for whom hell hath no fury... like. And I feel the first stinger stab next to my right eye.

Here's the thing about bees. Yes, all the ones who sting you are girls- and yes, they will sting you, even if you are Zen. But, more importantly -they are big into smells and if they smell that one of their crew is stinging they all join the party. All for one and one for all. Bees are a bit French.

So the pheromones are pumping and I have been stung... on the face. It's war. But, I'm still holding a box of bees. I exercise the most self-control of my life by slowly setting the box down as numerous stings being piercing my face. My eyes are screwed shut and I feel the box touch the ground. I throw my hands to my face, trying to protect it and I break out in a mad run toward my house.

Now here's the thing: What do you do? I'm under siege. I have been stung well into the teens at this point and a swarm of bees surrounds my head. I have killed a few bees as I slapped my hands to my face, I have begun an insane sprint toward my home, I'm losing some of the bees – but I honestly can't figure out where to go? I can't run indoors-my children are in there! I can't completely outrun them. They are in my hair, in my clothes on my hands and face.

A desperate shriek is coming from my mouth. This shriek is an attempt to alert my family to my predicament, and perhaps get some help. It was loud – desperate – braying. It was... impressive.

The mad sprint is not well executed. I lost shoes at some point - and sanity... and the sound pouring from my mouth falls between the shriek of a vixen and a cow getting branded. My brain determines that water is the best solution and a run around my home places me near a water spigot which I manage to turn on and stick my head under.

Bees stuck in your hair, attempting to sting you sound kinda funny when they're getting drowned in the faucet. It's *bzzzzzzz.z.....lllrlrlrrrbrbbbbbb*. More or less. And yes, you do have the presence of mind to think,"Huh, that's a funny noise."

My family – alerted by my howls and thrashing come outside to see what I'm doing. They get stung.

There is some swatting and more water. My husband might have laughed. And given me a Benadryl. And told me if I was allergic I'd be dead (see I told you!) And we pulled stingers out of everyone.

Then, think about this life lesson Zen masters: I was stung twenty some odd times, and yet I had to suit up in my bee suit, (like some lame, old, American beekeeper), act like I wasn't a baby – and go back to the hive and finish my job. That's a profound life lesson there! That's the sound of one hand clapping. And if it's not, it ought to be. 'Merica.

I was not finished with my bee inspired path to enlightenment, however. Have you ever seen someone who has been stung on the face? Even one time can usually cause a bit of swelling. Twenty-some times - mostly on the face... I want you to imagine what it would look like. (If you need help Bear Grylls has a Youtube video.) I looked like I had exploded internally- and my insides were trying to get outside – of my head.

Sometimes people can't control their expressions. I walked into a gas station a few days later. A man smiled and held a door for me. I looked up and thanked him. He jumped and made a weird noise deep in his throat. Just another step on my road to enlightenment! I gave numerous people opportunities in the ancient art of not responding negatively to an unsightly person. And, I think this was big of me -bringing balance and good energy to the world. I've grown through my adversity. I am certainly more enlightened. But, I'm also wearing a bee suit now... (and a bra.)

THANKSGIVING THEATRICS

There is tension in the air, so much is at stake, and the odds are not in our favor. For a good twenty years now I have been the provider of the turkey for the Thanksgiving meal, and these twenty years have taught us that, whatever talents God may have bestowed upon me, cooking isn't among them. Everything smells ok – but everyone is glancing anxiously my way - we know how often things have gone south before.

I'm trying to focus on the currently perfect turkey, but I'm acutely aware of a potential disaster... well a few, actually. Aunt Jenny is way too far ahead of the pack in her consumption of alcohol. We tried to hide the hooch until dinner was served to keep her from getting obnoxious, but she decided to bring her own, of course. The other concern is a fuzzy grey creature that I saw dart across the kitchen floor a few nights ago. There is a mouse. Somewhere. My brother and his wife are fancy lawyers from DC. This is not something I need them to see. Not just because she is pretentious and condescending towards everyone, which she is, but because Uncle Billy is just as pretentious and determined to preach the gospel of open spaces and Elk hunting, in detail, whenever she is within earshot. My family spends a decent part of the evening keeping those two separated at all costs.

I spot little teeny mouse droppings in a drawer. How in the heck did the mouse get into a drawer? Now I can't use any of the silverware that was in there – unless I want to give someone Hantavirus, which, since I'm pretty sure Aunt Jenny is currently trying to teach my seven-year-old how to twerk, I may be tempted. (Twerking is a dance with excessive, inappropriate, rear-end wiggling.) Of course, the second I toss a drawer full of silverware into the sink full of soapy water my stinking sister in law saunters up and ask what I'm doing. I laugh and ask her if I should be worried about whatever Aunt Jenny has our kids doing. An appalled expression crosses the pretentious face and she runs across the room. Boom – handled – maybe Aunt Jenny's drinking issues will prove useful for a bit.

Uncle Billy is loudly recounting a pheasant hunt in vivid detail while pointedly staring across the room, mostly at my sister-in-law but sometimes glaring at my brother for being a sellout. Uncle Billy has completely lost the interest of anyone around him, but he has no idea since he isn't even looking at them.

My little daughter has quit attempting to twerk with her aunt, but my four-year-old nephew is getting the hang of it. Aunt Jenny is doing some weird strut with a bouncing shaking rear end with my four-year-old nephew in tow – I do not think the coffeehouse tunes on the radio are working with their dance moves.

I see a grey flicker in the corner of my eye as I finish washing silverware, I whip my head, but the mouse is already behind the fridge. Dang! I don't know what I will do if I corner it anyway. How will my sister in law handle the BB gun getting fired in the house? The lecture on her lack of support for certain amendments in the Constitution is not going to go well.

My teenage daughter finally gets her face out of her phone, she runs to me crying, "He says we're done, Mom!!" I try not to roll my eyes and grab her in a quick hug... I'm honestly not too worried; her teenage romance has been nothing if not dramatic. They've been "done" four times already.

"Go make a pot of coffee, honey. Your Aunt Jenny needs some."

The turkey!!!! I smell a burnt smell!

I throw open the oven to a billow of smoke. I'm terrified, but it's ok – some of the stuffing just fell out and burned to the bottom of the oven. Everything is fine – the plastic doodad has popped, and we can get the bird on the counter.

Aunt Jenny has wandered into the kitchen. She's kind of twerking... kind of trying to help me with the gravy. I always ruin the gravy. EVERY. SINGLE. YEAR.

I start gently sifting and whisking flour into the pan the way Martha Stewart showed me on YouTube. I will get it right this time! I see Aunt Jenny head over to my sniffling daughter as she pours coffee beans. My husband is cleaning something out of the sink. I am slowly- slowly trying to move the hot turkey from the roasting pan onto a serving tray. It's slipping around on the rack and I know, I just know, a stinking mouse is going to run across my foot any second and I will lose my mind I swear I will! I lift... a leg appears to be slipping from the strings... I got it... I shift the bird – Aunt Jenny has completely abandoned the gravy and it's smoking. I yell to my daughter to turn off the burner. My husband's irritated face is beading with sweat as he messes with the disposal – what on earth is he doing?

I ONLY HAVE six inches to go. The turkey is wobbling, my daughter grabs the front wing area with a dirty oven mitt and saves the day we gently set the turkey down. Suddenly there's a loud grinding sound and my husband shrieks, yanks his arm from the disposal and thrusts it in the air! I scream suddenly realizing what must have happened!

We both stare in horror at his hand fresh from the disposal...

It's fine – there's nothing...??? What's going on?

I look to the corner – Aunt Jenny is doubled over with laughter as she holds the coffee grinder to her chest. We have got to sober that woman up.

I pull out the jars of gravy... another year of ruined gravy. The turkey is ok; I'm pretty sure. I ask myself a hundred times if I got all the weird stuff out of the turkey? I got the neck – and the baggy of stuff... and the other baggy... I got it all. No one's going to be shocked.

The counter slowly fills with all the sides. Potatoes, sweet potatoes, veggies. Uncle Billy keeps trying to sit near my brother. My nephew is holding court with at least half the room obsessed with his bottom as he bounces it around. I hear my daughter gasp staring at her cell phone, "Oh...! He's done with his Thanksgiving dinner!!!" She's beaming. Her whirlwind romance is saved... again. Aunt Jenny is still giggling and teasing my husband. He's just so happy to have a functional hand he could care less. We did it! Everyone will eat a pretty yummy Thanksgiving meal despite the jars of gravy.

We settle into seats and I talk my three-year-old niece

into doing our family prayer. This brilliant move always saves us from a heated religious debate where Uncle Tom decides to insult everyone of faith with his discussions of the invisible-flying-spaghetti-monster god. Uncle Tom isn't going to insult his little granddaughter though, and I use that against him. She mutters the sweetest most bizarre prayer, thanking God for peas and that her sister isn't really a werewolf and something about getting a gooey for Christmas? Eventually, someone says, "Amen" loudly and so she does as well.

Food is passed. Hugs and laughter are shared. I am a housewife hero bringing familial spirit and joy to all around with my tremendous food making/people pleasing skills. I bask in the glow of my success. Then a shriek rings out. "Is that a mouse?"

Chair screech sounds across the floor and Uncle Bill yells, "Where's the BB gun?"

*Names and situations have been changed (completely fictionalized) to protect the innocent. (Keep me from being kicked out of family gatherings).

** No mice were harmed in the writing of this column

THERE IS TOO MUCH WASTED, USELESS, TALENT IN THIS WORLD – AND I KNOW WHAT WE NEED.

Do you know that there are 7.5 billion people alive today? 7.5 Billion. I hear that number, and I cannot help but think of all that talent! All the great things that may be discovered!

But, I then wonder, how many of them are actually inventing things? Like zero! (Maybe a bit more... maybe like 5.) Not enough. I have some things that I am really hoping will be invented, and none of these 7.5 billion people are stepping up.

I blame video games. That's all that anyone is inventing- and then, anyone else who might invent something else is too busy playing the videos games they keep inventing. Video games are useless for me. I don't play video games. (It takes too much time from my important online complaining.) Did you know that there is a game where you steal cars and beat up people and that's all that you do? I'm not kidding. It's a game. Really. You can just go and buy a game where you act like a horrible, horrible person – and people love to play it. It's very popular.

I can't decide if I'm supposed to be happy that there's a

game that allows these people act on all the horrible stuff they apparently enjoy doing... assuming it keeps their awful desires virtual? Or should I just be really depressed that so many people are so jacked up? (I'll fall back on my usual... sit back in self-righteous shock and indignation as I recognize that I am clearly morally and ethically superior to vast swaths of society.) Now, from my pious position, I shall complain further about what these billions of humans should have done with their time instead of inventing video games.

Invent me a pill!!! Specifically, I want a nap – in a pill. and I want it to feel just like a nice long nap. I want a bottle of 50 and I want it delivered next day with free shipping. And, while you billions of people are doing useful things like this, I'd like to add a workout pill too. One of the ones where you get really sweaty and feel really sore the next day. I'd be ok getting wheezy and unable to walk up the stairs the next day, just so long as it came in a pill.

But, there is no nap in pill form, no workout in a bottle. They keep finding all sort of pills they will invent though... Did you know that they have invented anti-depressant pills that you take when your anti-depressant pills are too depressing? This is true. They invented anti-depressant anti-depressants. Can't get a decent nap in a bottle though.

You know what else? There are things called fidget spinners that the kids these days spin. (Apparently, a dradle isn't good enough). In fact, if you have ADHD and need to spin stuff, you can spin a fidget spinner ...medicinally. (I bet if you could get in more naps and exercise you'd need a lot fewer fidget spinners – and anti-depressant anti-depressants)

Imagine with me... if you will:

"Hey, Sarah. How are you?"

"I'm kind of tired, Lynn. I am going to go pop a couple naps and then take my test."

"Cool, I'd like the take a few edible workouts before I hit the pool. Get a pump on. Get swol." (That's a thing too... pretty sure)

But, alas it's just a dream.

You know what isn't a dream? There is an app on my kid's phone called "musical.ly." It involves lip synching while you video yourself and then sharing it to all the other people who were wanting to watch you lip synch! They invented that. It's hugely popular. Two million downloads. But – has that bought you a single second of sleep? No it hasn't. We have to sleep for a third of our lives. Think of what a nap in pill form could do! That could save a lot of sleeping. We could save impressive amounts of time by bottling that stuff! How come these people aren't making it a priority? Come on all you genius 7.5 billion. Just think, with all that time saved, you could play more videos games!

THE ART AND SCIENCE OF #2

I am dehydrated. Maybe not right this second, but I do spend a large portion of my time dehydrated. This is because I rock climb. Or, to be more accurate – my husband rock-climbs. I chit-chat and hold the rope while spending most of my time on terra firma. You see the rock-climbing, the hiking, the sun... none of that is the reason that I am dehydrated. No – I'm dehydrated because I hate having to pee out in the boonies.

I have been camping since I was a child, like many of you, and the solution for bathroom issues was a hole in the ground and toilet paper with a lighter. 1980's baby. Hair bands, hot pink, and traditional camping poop routines.

That's not how it is anymore.

Rock climbing, while still fairly obscure, has grown in popularity. Areas that we were climbing in 20 years ago, where you would never meet a soul, are now abuzz with the new hipster community. They are way more into safety than we were. They are adamant about helmet use, smart wool, and gortex. And they brought with them a million new ideas about how to go to the loo in the 'out of doors.'

The first thing I saw that clued me into the crazy new world came as a "gift" from my husband. It's called a "Go Girl." This thing... oh my goodness. I cannot even. He gave me a girly parts funnel! So a girl can "go" standing up, like a boy. This is a thing. He says it was a joke... but, I wonder. A girl funnel - just so I can camp and climb with the boys. If you want to talk sexism and the inequality of blah blah blah... I'm generally not interested. But, when it comes to handling business in mother nature no one is trying to design contraptions for men to make bathrooms issues more convenient. God gave them a funnel. That's real discrimination.

I was firm in the, "I will not be using a pee funnel... but thanks," and it sits forlornly never to be used. But, that is not the only issue with 'going' outside. Male or female, you have to number two - too. That was no big thing twenty years ago when "Friends" was new and rock climbers were weird. Now, climbing is cool, and climbing areas are dealing with too much poo - in too small an area.

I'm sure you have seen heated contentious online debates. Right vs. Left. Red vs. Blue. Atheist vs. Born Again vs. Hipster Spiritualist. It can be weird; different clubs become strange bedfellows in the 'enemy of my enemy' scenarios. Rock Climbers have debates as well. These are beyond boring and bizarre to the uninitiated (and normal). Which gear is best, why helmets are a must – why ropes are not a must. It's a weird world with fanatical opinions the likes of Comicon fans debating Star Trek vs. Star Wars. Topics for climber debates have managed to include the best way to handle number 2.

There is the 'dig a hole' group, in an argument with the 'some dog named "Canyon" with a hankie tied around his neck will just dig it back up' belief. There is the 'burn your toilet paper' club, but there is also the 'you will start a forest fire' (...in the desert) club. A solution has come in the form of a "wag-bag." This is a bag with kitty litter that you "use"- and you "hike out." This is what has happened to us in twenty years. You – carry your own poop around... for sanitary reasons. I know.

On the one hand... yay- less poop to bump into. But, isn't poop just fertilizer by another name? Doesn't it actually belong on the ground? Aren't all the animals going there? Isn't that what mother-nature intended? Granted, the animals aren't all piled up next to a cliff side, and also acknowledged, poop is full of bacteria and Giardia and will kill you. Still, why is playing outside so hard?

You know what you never see on a Patagonia ad? **Get outside... and carry your poop with you in a bag! Go outdoors... you can just pee in a funnel! Camping is awesome! Campfires, s'mores, guitars, stars, poop bags!** (Somehow, we just totally skip this.)

The wag-bag will be a good solution for all of you. It seems to be the most reasonable option. Good luck with that. It's not the option I have chosen.

When toilets get scarce – I go with my gut. Meaning, of course, I avoid using my gut – or bladder. I'll eat and drink when I know toilets are available, and until then, hunger and dehydration. It works – and I'm happy with that.

NON-MORNING PEOPLE

I hate mornings. No really. Like really really. When my consciousness first enters this terrestrial realm to the blaring of my alarm clock, I arrive wanting to punch someone. I enter this place in a rage - hoping to cause harm. That's just the truth. That is the world in the mind of non-morning people (to be known henceforth as NMPs). And it doesn't go away. The sensation of rage only dissipates with time and coffee... lots of both.

The BBC had a recent article on the genetic components that lead people toward being more alert in the mornings or evenings. They found that morning people tend to be more "persistent, self-directed and agreeable. They set more goals and have a better sense of wellbeing." However, there were a few benefits for NMPs: they tend to score slightly better on measures of memory and cognitive ability. The benefits for night people seem more limited, however. A study of professional baseball players found that morning players did have poorer batting averages when playing at night, but night owl baseball players did much worse when batting in the morning.

So, one might ask why on earth has Darwinian survival of the fittest not killed off our kind? Why do we still exist when we fit into all y'alls morning world so poorly? Well, I'm betting that plenty of wartime ambushes and important stuff went down at night when the enemy expected everyone to be asleep. But, not everyone was asleep. Grumk, the caveman, was still wide awake having a rough time falling asleep (as all NMPs do) and he heard the ambush coming and got his crew out of harm's way. Boom. Non-morning people win! So much genetic, evolutionary winning! (So that we can continue to exist in the world where we are constantly forced to wake up to alarm clocks at ungodly hours.)

Did it ever occur to you that humans are the only animal who goes to sleep when she is not tired and wakes up when she is? That seems so illogical. Why can a bird with no opposable thumbs, and a brain that is smaller than my big toe get to sleep in until she darn well pleases and I need to drag through ridiculous hours of misery every morning to please the public school system, and every job I ever had?

The other morning I was picking up coffee from Coffee Trader for the Little Indians Wrestling Tournament. (Hi Phong, Dee, Derek... wassup?) And you know what? There were people there acting all chipper and morningish. A guy in five finger shoes was jogging in, already done working out for the day. Jogging... before the sun had even bothered to wake up... in January!!!! I mean, if that isn't insane - well, I don't know what sanity is!! And there wasn't just the one guy, customers were in there, and the teenagers working there were all cute and happy – acting like the world doesn't suck at 7 am. It was a nightmare of alert, smiley, morning junkies watching the sunrise over steaming cups of joe. I hate them all.

I was a flight attendant in a former life and I had a route one month that started off in Raleigh North Carolina. The flight left at 5 a.m. That meant I needed to be on the plane setting up at 4 a.m. That meant I had to leave the hotel at 3:30 am – so I had to wake up at 2:30 am. I was based in California. 2:30 am in North Carolina is 11:30pm in California. Not gonna lie... I started waking up at 3:15 North Carolina time by the end of the month. Yes – really.

People from North Carolina who were my people (NMPs) would get on the plane and look at me smiling my flight attendant smile and say, "How can you be so happy at this hour?" And I would smile back at them as we both secretly thought about how we would like to punch each other. Because that's how NMPs feel. We feel mean... borderline violent... until 10 am. But – thank goodness, we are not violent, because we are too exhausted. While we may want to punch everyone... we want to close our eyes and ignore you - So. Much. More. We are actually quite benign. When approaching an NMP just give us a wide birth and watch us stumble from irritation to irritation with our eyes half closed.

Yes, we make you look good with our total incompetence. And yes you will make more money and be more successful in this life for your ability to wake up and enjoy your morning. But, I just want to remind you – we do fill an important role with our ability to be alert during the night time. Your late night trip to the ER, or a cross-Atlantic flight... there are some jobs you really want night people for. Think of this: the Minute Men of the Revolutionary War... We gotta assume those were some NMPs. That's right. Paul Revere riding through town screaming that the redcoats were coming? – He wasn't going to bed with the sun was he? So there you go, thanks to night people you survived a British attack and won the Revolutionary War. Bazinga – America. Your welcome.

Now leave me alone and let me go back to sleep.

MENTAL HEALTH EXPERTISE

So this month's column we are going to discuss mental health. Which is excellent. Because I am a great candidate by which one would choose to discuss mental health.

I am very healthy - mentally. I am almost a walking tribute to being healthy—mentally.

I certainly wouldn't feel insecure about my mental status.

I don't question, for example, purely hypothetically, if some of our readers may have heard me freaking out at my children in the City Market parking lot last month. Because I am pretty sure, that it didn't happen.

And if it did, or if I appeared a bit unkempt- or loud, it would only be because I did, in fact, tell those children a million times that they have to keep their drinks in the cup holders and could not keep setting the drink in their laps! And that if they kept setting the drinks in their laps and managed to spill those stupid, sticky, drinks all over the minivan - that I desperately want to keep from reeking of stale french-fries and sadness – that I would lose my mind! Then, let's just assume, they DID set their drinks in their laps and they DID manage to spill sticky fluid into every crease of this stupid Mom van that DOES smell to high heaven it would only make sense, in a situation such as that, for a person to be a bit flustered... and I may have appeared a bit flustered to a few of you who happened to have seen me in the parking lot last month. Perhaps.

I ALSO, am-in-no-way worried, that you might question my mental stability when I am a spectator at my kids sporting events. I don't think I have made a fool of myself in front of some of you, at times, in that arena. For example: at my child's wrestling match? I doubt it has happened that I, perhaps, started yelling at my sweet, gentle, son to do violent acts to the child he is engaged in a match.

I DON'T WORRY that you may have seen me smiling and negotiating the floors of Montrose High School's gymnasium quiet and serene (as I always am...) and then (upon realizing my son was three points down in a match) suddenly dropping to my knees, sweat beading on my cheeks, pretty new necklace from JC Penny's flying into my hair as I get, maybe, a bit drool-y and shout-y in encouraging my child to take another woman's child and throw him onto his back like a bug and squeeze him until he BREAKS!!!!!!

BECAUSE THAT'S a bit trashy and lacking in self-control... and I wouldn't be the kind of woman who would do such a thing. Such a woman might find herself trying to stand up off the matt and compose herself in front of the entire community, after flailing and screeching like a lunatic over a silly wrestling match. These are just kids after all, this is just for fun. No one's going to the Olympics here. I mean... obviously – we are dignified.

And, honestly, the last thing I would be worried about is anyone in this town questioning, not just my sanity, but my overall lack of intelligence, if I were to...(just spit balling here...) get lost trying to find, say, my child's school.

I mean, I take them to school 5 days a week... for years. So I couldn't get lost, just because, let's say, I got distracted by a Podcast and drove right past it... three times. And then had to explain that my child was late... again.

I MIGHT NOT BE A LIAR, but you can imagine why I might not want to divulge that I was distracted and drove right past the school. Three times. Again.

Because what kind of person is that easily distracted? Who has that little ability to focus on the task at hand? A person like that might need medication or some sort of ADD drugs or an IQ test. So, I clearly wouldn't be worried that this is something any of our readers might know about me... or be thinking about me as they ponder my ability to write with any authority on a subject like mental health.

I am clearly a healthy person! Mentally. I mean, I have my little quirks. Don't we all though, really? My little meltdowns or distractions are just fine. I can discuss mental health without anyone thinking it's awkward or inappropriate.

. . .

On the whole, I'm good. Solid. My brain is on firm footing. Metaphorically. It's not like I think brains have feet or anything. Ha!

I'm not crazy!

TURKEY TALK

THANKSGIVING... THE GIVING OF THANKS. A TIME WHEN we all remember to be a grateful people; to focus on the many blessings around us that we so often forget.

We are grateful for our turkey, assuming it's not dry and isn't still raw, and no one accidentally left the neck in the butt... because who would ever do that? No one, obviously. That's weird.

But, on the subject... Why do they stick a neck in the butt of the turkey? I mean, why is that where they put it? And the giblets... why are they on the other side? Why not put everything in the same end? Is there a reason? Or was one guy just trying to figure out where to shove some of the leftover odds and ends (that the cool people like Marth Stewart use to make soup or something, but the rest of us just feed to the cats), and he said: "Hey, I know – I'll stick these things up here, and this neck... I'll stick it in the butt. And then I'll freeze the whole thing!"

Then even though you've been thawing the big bird in your fridge (taking up all the space that you need to be filling with the holiday sides that Martha Stewart told you that you should make ahead, but you can't - BECAUSE the turkey is taking up all that space thawing!) when you swear it has thawed enough - you still can't get the darned neck out because it's still frozen to the turkey's internal cavity! And then your hands are throbbing in pain and cold when you try to pry it out and then... maybe... it winds up just getting thrown in the oven with the turkey because for sure you'll remember to pull it out later and not forget and leave it... that would be... ummm, kinda gross.

Did that guy decide to just toss the neck in the one end and the rest in the other end and everyone else has just followed suit believing he had a great reason behind his choice? Is it possible that he had no rhyme or reason and to this day we have a turkey neck in the turkey butt... for no real reason?

Interesting side note. Would you like to know what happens if you google that question – or really anything about turkey necks?? Google decides you need a facelift. That's what. Now I keep getting ads telling me about surgeons who can fix my turkey neck. Google is hurting my feelings.

And we are grateful that the roadwork in town is finally getting finished (Obviously, when Thanksgiving arrives it will be finished.) Because it's about time we could actually drive two blocks without another flipping detour and I'm sure by November we will be able to drive down a single street in this town without getting rerouted, or worse pulled over for speeding, because we are twenty minutes late because we were stuck in roadwork. I mean, they have got to get it finished! So we can start driving in the ice and snow.

We are also grateful that someone brought jars of gravy - when the gravy winds up lumpy and burned... again. We are grateful, though we all try to pretend that we like our gravy lumpy and burned. I can't tell you how grateful we are for jars of gravy even though suddenly everyone actually declares that they think smoky gravy is nice, and they always liked their gravy lumpy. But somehow, everyone still winds up eating the grocery store brand jars of gravy.

How many times have I been told that people like their gravy lumpy and burned? Nobody likes their gravy that way! It's not smoky... it tastes like cigarettes. Yes... someone... (me) ruined it again. Let's pop open the jars and make a joke and move on. Someday we can be grateful for homemade gravy but this year will not be the year; next year isn't likely either.

And we are grateful for butter. Because that's really the secret to all of Thanksgiving. 'Just put more butter in it,' ...in the turkey, in the gravy, in the pie, in the potatoes. More butter. Just add more butter. Maybe not to the cranberries... or you know what... maybe? Who knows? It's never failed. More butter is the answer, regardless of the question.

But, let's be honest. We aren't really all that grateful for the food... the food is good, but we are spoiled. We eat - all day -every day. We know nothing of children starving to death, or the old or broken unable to find bread. No, we are shamed with plenty. We are not grateful for the shelter... it's a given. Humble perhaps, donated by a church or the government possibly, but shelter is an achievable goal.

What we truly must be grateful for, is the greatest need in all of history, for all people, at all times. It is not that we have our basic needs met, or even that we have our palette delighted. It is that we have people.

This time of year we must be grateful for people who care for us, the people that we care for. People who are kind to us, and honest with us. People who tell us what we need to hear, and comfort us when we need that too. Because no delicacy, or fine dining experience, is of any value at all without someone to share it with. And in pure truth, there is nothing more difficult in this world than becoming a person of character and heart and finding other such people to join in your tribe. Not perfect people, but kind people; not brilliant, or accomplished, or talented, though that is nice enough, of course. We must locate the kind, good, honest, hardworking, generous and loving. These people are hard to find - they are even harder to be.

So, after you burn your gravy, discover frozen necks in your turkey butt, gnaw on dense flat rolls that never managed to rise...then look around your table. And if you know the people looking back at you are people who love you dearly, then eat that rock, solid, bread roll with delight. Money, success, talent, time... nothing can buy the joy of good friends and family. Those are a gift you must earn yourself and give to yourself. And for that, you must be grateful.

PARENTING IS NOT A SIDE ISSUE

"Remember that children, marriages, and flower gardens reflect the kind of care they get."

— H. Jackson Brown Jr.

Most weekdays you will find me in an office downtown, working with kids who have lost access to their parents. Sometimes it's not that big of a deal – it's a custody dispute that's getting out of hand or a kid who really did just take a nose dive down a flight of stairs. But, most of the time – it is a kid whose life is going to be a whole lot worse because he was born to the wrong people. Most of the time, I can prove statistically, if he'd had a Mom who was sober, a Dad who was around – he would lead a happy, healthy, loving, productive life – and yet with the hand he was actually dealt; prison, teen pregnancy, and abuse are in his future.

And yes, these are the extremes – but even within the

margins of "normal", it is so important to remember that people don't just become adults. Children are raised. They are tended to. I don't know why, but these days there is very little interest in the art of parenting. We spend hours watching cooking shows, gardening, hunting, home renovation. Why are we not as passionate and interested in the art of rearing good human beings? They don't just show up in a business suit with a job. Someone makes choices, all day, every day, that completely affect the trajectory of that child's life. People must learn to be honest, kind, helpful, gracious, patient, good. They are taught these things. They learn that these behaviors are expected in their home, and in their community. When they meet dishonesty or cruelty, it should register with shock because that is not how they know the world to be designed.

I can attest that kids also learn deceit, cruelty, impatience, addiction. If that is the world they experience, they will mold themselves to the same behavior.

The most thought-provoking book I've read in the past decade is called, "The Marshmallow Project." It is a book based on decades of studying children and self-control. The kids in the program were offered a marshmallow now, or two marshmallows if they could wait. The authors of the study then followed these kids well into their adult lives. The correlation between a child's ability to wait to receive two marshmallows and his success in life was shocking.

Guess what made the biggest difference between a child who could wait and one who could not? No surprise - it was family life. Active, involved parents were teaching their children patience – but more than that they were teaching them trust. If they had a mother who followed through on what she said, the children could wait. If a father could be depended on when he said there would be a punishment or a reward – those kids were comfortable waiting. But, if they didn't trust their parents to follow through, they didn't trust that the second marshmallow was worth the risk of skipping the one they could have now. If Dad never is around, never plays with me as he promised – then I learn that I should take the good things while I have the chance. And this little belief – this little idea about how the world works, becomes a huge issue as an adult. A tiny belief about trust has a trajectory that will play out in a dramatic way in a child's future.

WE NEED to start holding parenting to a higher station. We need to recognize how profound, beautiful, important, and irreplaceable the role of parents truly is. I know life is busy and crammed to the gills... mine is and it's something I'm personally battling... but parenting can't be the side issue in life – it needs to be the primary issue.

At CASA I am watching daily the slow destruction of innocent people on their road to adulthood. It's apparent over and over and over that kids are needy. They are not a low maintenance gig. A child needs chronic, constant, daily, incessant love. They need to be the absolute joy of someone's life. That's not a negligible issue to a child. They have to matter more than anything, more than a boyfriend, or booze, or jobs, or friends. They need to be the whole world to someone. And when they are not – when they are the side dish on a full plate... it changes them.

BENJAMIN FRANKLIN ONCE SAID, "Educate your children to self-control, to the habit of holding passion and prejudice and evil tendencies subject to an upright and reasoning will, and you have done much to abolish misery from their future and crimes from society." Every day I see this played out in real time. As much as I'd love to find that in my work I can fix all the damage done to children in their early years, the truth is – this is a lesson that must be taught at home. Trust and security can't be given to a child anywhere else if it isn't given from a loving home. I'd like it if those of us in foster care could make a product that could be the perfect band-aid for: "Your parents were sucky." But there is no band-aid. Parents ARE the only source for these lessons. And honestly, why be anything but the best dang parent you can possibly be?

JUST DO IT... FOR YOUR HEART.

THIS MONTH VALLEY HEALTH IS FOCUSING ON HEART health.

I hate to disappoint you, dear readers... but I am not a cardiologist.

Sorry.

But, I've done some excellent research. I went to Google, and I googled a bunch of stuff - about hearts and cardiovascular systems. I googled about strokes and DNA links, and then I asked a few medical people I know, followed by a few fun TED talks – they may or may not have been entirely unrelated.

Here's what I found out:

#1. A decent chunk of heart health is related to DNA. You may have certain pre-disposition to a bad heart. You can't do anything about that.

#2. Some more obvious lifestyle factors affect your heart. If you are overweight, your heart and circulation are taking a beating on behalf of your stomach. Quit being a jerk to your heart. It's not nice.

But, there is something else – that is actually a huge factor in your cardiovascular health...

#3. Your attitude and ability to manage stress also are impacting your heart.

Example: When a car cuts you off in the overwhelming traffic of Montrose... (That's a joke – if you are stressed out in Montrose traffic then you are a weenie and need to go spend a week on the 405 in LA at six o'clock before you are allowed back into the city limits. I'm serious.)

Back to you getting cut off... A car has cut you off while you're cruising down Rio-Grande and you get mad. Really mad. "What the heck?!?" you think.

You give them a gesture that your mom would slap you for. You think dark, evil, thoughts toward their bumper sticker, which, of course, represents a political party that you despise!

Then you wander into that Montrose High School basketball game while muttering exotic curses worthy of great Irish men of yore... "May the wind be ever in your face and may your brake pads wear early and uneven!!!"

This situation, you may be shocked to discover, is not great for your heart. It may be even more shocking to discover that the problem is not actually the guy who pulled out in front of you. The problem is... wait for it.... You! You are the big, fat, problem here.

This in no way applies to me by the way. I never get mad at other drivers. I am a zen master capable of blessing those who curse me. Much like Mother Theresa, my mentor in all situations road rage related.

But you... you have an issue. You are killing your poor heart by being so incapable of coping with stress. Fortunately for you there are solutions.

The first one is to get involved in a faith community. People who practice faith live longer, healthier, happier lives. They spend a significant amount of time learning to see the positive in life and support one another in difficult times.

I won't tell you which community you should join... I will simply let you know that I am part of the good one and all the other ones are really bad. (That's a joke – if it offended you then that was bad for your heart too.)

You also should spend more time giving out hugs. When people hug, (and not just other people, hugging your cat or dog works too), their stress hormones dissipate, and their blood pressure drops immediately. The other great thing about hugging is that it establishes bonds that last even longer. So a hug today means more hugs down the line, and all hugs are heart medicine! Did you get that? Heart medicine = hugs. Do it!

Another thing you need to do more of. Laugh.

Laughter has an immediate impact on vasoconstriction. A laugh will immediately relieve many symptoms of stress; it releases feel-good hormones and builds the immune system.

How do you go about laughing? Well, I have a few suggestions.

I was recently advised that you can ask Siri to beatbox for you. I found it effective.

My teenager also thinks Siri is amusing to ask questions regarding the mixing of dog breeds like Shitzu with, well ... pretty much any breed. Example: What do you call a Shitzu breed with a Poodle... and so on and so forth.

In order to do good thorough research in the area of laughter and heart health I recognized that I must self-experiment. (The things I do for you!) I made myself sit down and watch as much funny stuff as I could on the internet. It had to be done.

I suffered through clips of people falling a lot. I found a car embedded in the side of a building. (Can you picture that?? It's just a car sticking halfway out of the wall of a building.)

There were the always funny people coming out of anesthesia.

Here's a funny one. Google "sticky floor prank." It's a guy, dressed in a business suit. He enters a building in which, somehow, they have managed to lay a huge carpet made of flypaper across a floor. The whole thing takes less than a second. His hair gets stuck. It's hilarious.

I found Pinterest had images of people getting frightened in haunted houses. Teenage boys with their legs wrapped around their screaming mothers...

I also heard some fun real-world suggestions to get laughter going. One was to get into an elevator full of people and start doing tai chi... (this would probably help your heart in two ways.) The other suggestion was to face the rest of your fellow elevator mates instead of facing the door.

I can't decide if it would be funnier to just do this with a straight face or to plaster a big creepy smile on your face?

It might be even better to quote something you memorized while a kid. The preamble to the constitution or the "rap" you used to memorize the Pythagorean theorem.

I really hope I'm in the elevator with you when you try this out. I will be standing in that weird moment facing the door with a box full of strangers... you will be ready to go big for your heart. You will turn slowly around – everyone in the elevator will immediately become painfully uncomfortable. Then suddenly you will burst into a song about the states and their capitals... complete with hand gestures and perhaps an impromptu box step.

Please – PLEASE somebody do this for me! It will be so awesome I can't even stand thinking about it.

I also really love videos of infants cracking up when paper is ripped, or... ok... I admit it - I love watching children totally eat it on America's funniest home videos.

Don't judge.

I'm doing this for you. And here's the thing: you need to go and laugh at the falling children! Not because you are heartless Germanic schadenfreude(r) and find humor in their pain... you are doing this for your health. And hey... put the oxygen mask on yourself first – right? It's medicinal!

THE REAL REASON

EVERYTHING HAPPENS FOR A REASON. SOMETIMES THE reason is: You're stupid and you make bad decisions.

I love this. It's brilliant. I totally get the: There are no accidents" esoteric approach to life - but, I'm also a big believer in gravity. If you have a dumb idea – it will lead to... where it will lead to. So, I'm often tickled by the way in which you can look at failure and see the string of bad ideas that proceeded it.

Take Scotland. Scotland has been under the boot of England for, well, ever. But why? I mean – in Brave Heart the Scottish look to be bad mothers... right? All swarthy and blue and running around in skirts and whatnot. But they never seem to be able to kick those jerks, the English, to the curb.

In fact – let's give some credit where it's due. England has at times conquered almost half the world. Really. They took over India, Australia, Canada, a chunk of Africa, sometimes France, Italy, the Middle East... they were even the boss around here for a while.

But they are so tiny! They are this little island; not a lot of people—so how'd they get so powerful? And—why were so many people unable to defend their territories?

Well, Scotland, I think I may have found part of your problem. See—the national animal of England... is a lion. That's a tough animal. But, I know what you're thinking. They don't even have lions in England? Never have. I mean, I understand the lion for Israel—there were lions in the Middle East. England has no lions. But, this is England—they just go take the stuff they want. And—hey—at least when they picked an animal they looked around for a cool one. They didn't let a lack of actual relationship to their country deter them. Just like it didn't deter them from snapping up other cultures and land. We like lions! We're taking them. Done. (It's why we had to kick them out... they have issues.)

At least in our country we pick a native animal! The USA is symbolized by the Eagle. That's just cool. We always hear about Ben Franklin wanting the turkey. Thank goodness he lost that vote. A turkey? That's got to be the most pathetic animal a country could have. We'd be German by now for sure if we were running around lauding our country as the land of the turkey.

But – Scotland – they did it one better. Their national animal – to this day – is...

The unicorn.

So.

That's going to be a problem.

See – in choosing their animal back in the cold and dark times of whale oil lamps and typhoid they heard about how the unicorn could totally kick butt on a lion. So if England was a lion??? Well, they for sure would be a unicorn.

I'd say the irony here is pretty rich. Imaginary animals... they just have a hard time winning a battle against real animals... so... betting on the magical one seems like a poignant symbol of losing based on poor decisions and faulty information.

No—of course Scotland hasn't avoided conquering the world in the way that England did based solely on the fact that they picked a unicorn as their animal. But – there is some evidence that they spent way too much time trying to conquer one another – and too little time getting their crap together, in order to fight a common threat. Still, trusting a magical animal as a symbol of strength seems to fall in line with that.

Not that England is such a laudable tradition. They took over half the world... and in so doing... are hated by half the world. (We got over it – because we kicked them out.) Eagle vs lion - eagle wins?? Wings are helpful I suppose.

But, don't we all know a few folks out there choosing unicorns to lead the way? Sometimes a unicorn seems easier to believe in. Functional real world stuff is miserable. Sitting around with a bunch of people you can't stand to form a functional country that can move in a functional way... that is awful, and irritating, and exceptionally boring.

Why is it that good ideas are so tedious? Kale, running, PTA meetings?? Someday eating Enstrom Toffee and watching reality TV should accomplish something. That's when the unicorns win! And the turkeys will conquer! It will be the "Age of Aquarius" and such. Until then – sit through the long, boring meetings and go for a walk and eat a salad. For this is the stuff that lions are made of.

FAMILY BIRTHDAY PARTIES

I dropped my daughter off for a lesson recently and she was telling her instructor that it was her Dad's birthday that day. She then mentioned that it was almost her birthday as well, and then she remarked that everyone in her family would be having their birthdays soon. "My Mom is really stressed out," she added.

Yep. We are a family of five – and all of us are born in September.

Quit counting – it's Christmas.

Nine months before September is Christmas and yes – it appears to be the cause of our busy month. We, like, really really love the holidays.

So when school rolls around, not only am I preoccupied with three different kids going to three different schools which start and end at six very different times (you should all feel sorry for me and my mini-van now), but I am also trying to arrange for a very happy birthday for every single stinking person in this family.

It starts with my husband. What do you get men for

their birthdays? Seriously – I'm asking. I have never figured this out.

You can always get women something. Clothes, jewelry, a pedicure. Not men.

Let's face it, if a man wants something he goes out and gets it. And if he hasn't gotten it, it's because he can't afford it. My husband would love a big rock-climbing trip, a really nice car, or a new dirt bike. But we can't afford those things, and I promise you, if we could afford them – they would be ours currently. Most people are trying to get their loved ones gifts that actually work in a family budget. Let's assume $30-50. Maybe creeping into the very very low three digits if it's just the perfect gift.

Ummmm?? I think that leaves alcohol or coffee? (If you're a Mormon or 7th Day Adventist, one of those no coffee or alcohol faiths… I honestly can't imagine what you get men? Socks?!) We got him a baseball cap that doesn't fit and a coffee pot that he didn't want because he likes ours better.

Kids are easier. When celebrating birthdays for the kids we space a few gifts out over the course of the day. Open one before school, one after school, and a few after birthday cake that night. And they get the choice of food for dinner and breakfast. Done.

The only real advice I have to give on birthdays is this. Don't try to plan a party. Just don't.

If you plan a party at the park – it's going to rain. If you plan a party at home it will be a disaster and your home will be a mess. And I will show up to pick up my kids and wind up talking your ear off for an extra hour. Instead, you should combine all of your kid's birthdays into one big one and pay someone else to host it!

Go to Mack's Family Center, Black Canyon Gymnastics, the Rose Bowl, or the Montrose Rec Center pool and pay them to throw a party for you. It's the absolute best advice. They are the professionals. The kids will have fun – and then your daughter won't be telling the world what a stress case you are.

I suppose this is not as affordable for many of you who have to host a different party for each kid. If their birthdays are spread throughout the year – I guess I can't really help you. You probably should have given birth to all of your kids in one month. Clearly you don't enjoy Christmas enough.

TOO MUCH OR NOT ENOUGH?

Usually when I write articles I come at it from a place of knowledge. A lesson learned. I feel some experience, or wisdom has been gained and want to share... this is not that article.

This is a lost in the wilderness article. Wandering the desert for forty years – work in progress – still in the struggle – that kind.

I don't like not knowing things. I spend inordinate amounts of time researching, well – everything. I know everyone googles stuff every day – but I really do know that I'm a bit more obsessive than most. Something in the news about heart disease and saunas... I'm going to read the articles – then I'll read the medical journal the articles are based on – and decide if I really believe it was the sauna's heat that was responsible for the improved cardiac survivability or if I think it was the relaxation and socialization that are promoted by saunas that was actually responsible. It doesn't change anything – I'm still not going to spend time in a sauna... so why I feel the need to know is beyond me, but I like to KNOW.

I don't know how to raise a middle-schooler. I mean, I know how to feed him, to discipline him – heck – my kids don't really need discipline anymore. What I don't know, is how to help him become the best man he can be.

How much do you push – challenge? How much do you stand back and let them make their choices?

Great creative geniuses – the Steve Jobs – Bill Gates – Mark Zukkerburgs, they didn't become who they were because they followed the rules. They had to be free from obsessing about grades and classes and being good little academic robots. But, most of us aren't those guys—most of us do need good grades and to learn a trade or skill through some academic channel. If Steve Jobs had been my kid and wanted to take a calligraphy class?? Things would have gotten heated. Who's going to pay thousands for their kid to learn calligraphy? Buh-by Apple... pushy Mom killed it.

But, I know what lazy crap parenting results in. We could lie to ourselves and pretend that as long as kids have love they will be fine. And sure— many of us live lives that are... fine. But if you really LOVE your kids—you strive for them, you see their potential and encourage them. You give their talents and abilities the best possible opportunity to grow. Fruit trees can grow wild... but orchards take effort— and a parent has a responsibility to put effort and love into his/her kids.

So... Wednesday morning, get to school over an hour early—wrestling practice. A full day of school in which I expect notes to be constantly taken and updated so assignments aren't missed. If you get a B in this class your Mom will be disappointed in you—we both know you can do better. After school, stay to practice instruments. Then another wrestling session. Homework – and no you can't eat that!? How is that going to help you build muscle? But you need to eat more... you need lots of calories to grow. Get to bed earlier—you can't learn/grow if you don't get enough sleep – wake up early, you need to do chores before we get you to school.

Too much pressure? Too much investing into a kid? Not enough? Where's the line people? And is it different with each kid? Am I challenging him too much? Too interested in his athletic abilities, too obsessed with his academics? Too obsessed with his music? Not obsessing enough? Should we fix his mistakes for him more often? He's just a kid after all? But he won't ever learn if someone always helps him? How much responsibility is too much at 12? I am a wreck. I feel like we are over-scheduled and yet, he never gets these years back, and the lessons he learns today will be huge when he is an adult and there are full grown adults who haven't managed to figure out how to stay on top of their responsibilities, to get things finished on time, to be polite while under pressure, to clean up after themselves and think through difficult ideas and use their talents and strengths. If he doesn't learn these lessons soon, well, we've all seen what can happen.

No- I'm not asking you for advice. Well, maybe a little – but I'm not promising to take it. I have a feeling this will require some on the job training for me, and some of that obsessive research I like, and the advice from those Mom's who I admire. But – it is something I have been struggling with for months now, and I'm not finding a simple solution. This isn't going to be answered to my satisfaction after a few quick reads from a journal here or there... this is the life of my kid. My best buddy. The person I love and admire as much as anyone on the planet. I will not fail him; and one way or another, I will get this Mommy thing right. That is loving my kid – and man I really do.

THE MAMMALIAN DIVING REFLEX, YOU FORGOT YOU HAD ONE...

Just how long can a person hold their breath? One to two minutes... right? Why don't you stop reading right now – grab your phone's timer and check your own ability? I'll wait.

You didn't do it did you? That's ok – I wouldn't either. I hate holding my breath. It's like my body really wants me to breathe and makes the experience of not breathing feel rather unpleasant.

Because... of course.

Of course your body wants you to breathe. Of course you are designed to hate that feeling, to avoid it at any cost. You are a land mammal. You are designed to breathe constantly and walk around on the dusty dry ground... aren't you?

Actually, there is a lot of research that suggests you may not be.

Every person on the earth today carries within them the skills from a bygone ancestor – the mammalian dive reflex.

The mammalian dive reflex is a well-known reflex in all water mammals. It allows our otter friends to hold their breath for extended lengths of time with reflex bradycardia and peripheral vasoconstriction. These force blood from the extremities to be moved to their body's core, the heart can slow, sometimes in deep dives to as little as ten beats per minute, and the brain itself uses less oxygen while the spleen will release a store of oxygenated blood. The interesting thing about the mammalian dive reflex, is that it happens to all mammals... even us two-legged land lovers.

In fact, the dive reflex can be triggered without even entering the water. A bit of cold water splashed on your face can immediately trigger the reflex. It won't work if you stick your hand in the sink, or dip your toe in the pool, but the second your face is submerged your body transforms.

Your heart rate will drop substantially – from ten to twenty-five percent, and your body will shunt much of your blood to your vital organs and brain. In fact, while peripheral vasoconstriction often will only affect arterioles, in the case the of mammalian dive reflex all of the vasculatures is affected. The spleen may become involved as well, releasing a reservoir of oxygen-rich blood after protracted periods without oxygen. Your body, at all times, is just sitting on a system—prepped and ready to become a water animal, capable of existing without air exposure for far longer than we would assume.

There is a sport today that pursues nothing but pushing the limits of the mammalian dive reflex. (First world problems... finding a way to hold your breath... competitively.) These men and women push their bodies to the point of near death to find out just how deep into the ocean depths they can travel while holding their breath. It turns out – really deep, and really long.

The records set are mind-blowing. The current record for a male contestant holding his breath is 11 minutes and

35 seconds. The female record is currently 9 minutes and 5 seconds. The greatest depths reached are 281 and 237 meters respectively. (That's 307 yard and 257 yards - in American.) Think about that!!!! A man swam more than three football fields down into the ocean!! A man held his breath for nearly 12 minutes! That is mind-bending! Outside magazine journalist James Nestor spent a full year traveling and studying these accomplishments for his recent book "Deep." Not only were these competitive divers reaching unbelievable depths, but, he also studied societies that have been using these reflexes for hundreds, even thousands of years.

In Japan he followed the Ama, Japanese women who still dive every day for clams. While they don't have records of the amazing breath holding lengths we see competed for today, they would often spend over an hour at a time diving repeatedly for clams and even pearls. Usually going twice a day. These women live their daily lives as a sea mammal and have done this for thousands of years.

It is a bit mind-bending to research, especially when I struggle pitifully to hold my breath for a few seconds on the couch. (You get weird looks from your children too.) But it appears there is a version of humanity that we have lost. A version in which we are a cousin to the animals in the sea. As people, we have many of the same skills and techniques available to us that we assumed were unique to beavers or even orcas. An ancient memory still resides in our DNA, and we can awaken it, even now.

A TIME TO LAUGH, A TIME TO WEEP.

"This is a public service announcement: Just in case you are a parent of a senior and you haven't felt the need to cry about them graduating and leaving home, I just want you to know I've got you covered. And as luck would have it, I'm a sympathetic crier, so I'll cry for anyone. Mother of a first-born graduate
✔ *Single mom with a graduate*
✔ *Mother of only child who will graduate*
✔ *Mother of a child who graduated last year or next year*
✔ *Mother of newborn who will graduate in 18 years*
✔ *I can cry while I'm washing the dishes, driving or getting ready to teach. I'm your go-to girl for crying! So if you see me in this state, just shake your head sympathetically and keep walking, (that's what my boys do.) I'll get over myself someday. Probably when we start cleaning his room and my head explodes from all the crap in there. Until then..."*

— Amy Ayer Peebles - Mother of a graduating senior from Hotchkiss High School.

'Tis the season for crying. I have cried so many times in the past two weeks and I do not currently have a kid leaving the nest. My daughter did graduate from elementary school. Rang the bell at Cottonwood. I got emotional - I remember when her brother did the same. It's the time of year when all over town, well, all over the country, kids are crossing finish lines. College, Highschool all the way down to Pre-school... the season is ending, and we are marking time in a clear, definitive way. And for every parent, it's awfully painful to see the time passing so clearly. To see the change on the face of it.

So much of a child's growth happens in ways that we don't acknowledge. When was the last time I carried my son fast asleep from the car to bed? That happened with no trumpets or certificates. It was a big day – a huge change, and it was never marked. When was the last time my daughter fell asleep on me? The last time I carried her with her legs wrapped around me? When was the first day that they could hike faster than I could? Or beat me in a foot race? The day my son knew more about math than I did, or when my daughter was a better athlete? I think she was 7? When was the last time my kid ran to me when he got hurt instead of dealing with it independently?

These little milestones happen without the fanfare we'd like... the fanfare they honestly deserve. But, instead, we recognize the changing of school years – the final season of sports and diplomas completed. And we cry now – because all these other changes were achieved within these seasons, unnoticed until we look back. It's been such a beautiful, painful ride. I know that so many of you are sniffling along with Amy as we all take stock of the years. Looking at kids who no longer have those fat little fingers that fit deep into our hands. It all moves so quickly and quietly. I remember my Mother commenting on the day my youngest brother drove away from home for the first time. My Dad had given his kids a ride the mile down to the bus stop every single school day for over 18 years... and that morning he didn't have his job to do. She said he kept walking over to the window and looking out ... like there was something out there that he was forgetting. She said he seemed a bit lost. Never again would he have to do that drive. And just like that; A season ends. No fanfare – no diploma – no congratulations on nearly two decades of bus stop runs. Just – finished.

So this week, we feel it all. The weight of all the little conquests – first night in a big kid bed, the first black eye, the first time the kid grabs the phone and shows you how it's done, the first time you look up at them instead of down. All the little wins and changes. This is the week to stop and take it all in. And cry.

I'M SMART

I'm smart. Really. I know you may doubt this, I did as well. There is so much evidence to the contrary. I often get lost... on the way to drop my kids off at school. That's true, almost weekly. I will just start driving and at some point, one of my children will shout that we have arrived at the wrong school, or at Black Canyon Gymnastics (where we live half our lives) or even at a grocery store... somewhere my brain spazzed in my foggy minded state and we wander somewhere – but not to the school from which they will be receiving their education. And that's just one of the many ways you may have seen me behave foolishly.

I can get completely befuddled in a conversation that I don't understand and ask a question that is not just ill-informed, it's often obtuse. I will say with confidence something I believe to be relevant only to discover I should be embarrassed. For example, this happens regularly when I'm amongst medical people discussing something medical; I think I'm following along – then I add a small nibblet to the conversation and suddenly a pitying and amused glance steals across the faces in the room. I don't know what I said, but I know they are collectively trying not to laugh. This also happens when I discuss anything related to ranching-animal husbandry, or automotive mechanics, or technology... especially technology.

This is all true, and many of you know because you have been with me as I wander through this life a bit off in my knowledge. But, I discovered that for all my faults, I am smart. Not just smart; I think I may be cracking the top percentiles—borderline genius, because according to the news, which I found on the internet, I had my standards set way to high.

People are eating laundry soap. For fun. This is a real, true thing. Politicians are lobbying to make laundry soap look less fun to eat – to protect young adults from eating the stuff. For fun. I can't stress this enough. Today we have to protect people from eating laundry soap - as a form of entertainment. This is a problem in our world today!

This is crazy, but it is not the first time I have discovered my shocking levels of intelligence. I have seen warning signs for a whole lot of bizarre things. People are warning me not to use plastic grocery bags for baby bedding. I have to cut off warning labels on every single throw pillow in my home because apparently throw pillows are a source of life and death struggle for some folks and I must be warned. I have warnings on my ladder to avoid standing on the top rung. (I ignore this warning... I may be dumb, but I'm not uncoordinated) (You're supposed to laugh there... not write grumpy letters to the editor about the importance of safety). I also am aware that at least half of the speed limits in the city are clearly established for people with incredibly poor driving abilities, or to keep our law enforcement officials busy acting as hall monitors. I'm not sure which. But let's all be honest, for some reason we live in a town with some ridiculously low-speed limits, unmatched in the rest of the country and a law enforcement community with an unmatched zeal.

While I'm discussing my brilliance, I'd be amiss if not mentioning that I also have never thought it necessary to be informed that the little powder packet that came in the box of tennis shoes wasn't edible... and I didn't need to know all the warnings on household cleaning items that tell me I shouldn't marinate my chicken in them. (Except for the warnings about mixing bleach products with ammonia. Have you ever done that??!! That's rough – I need that warning label, still not smart enough to figure out which is which.)

So – over time, I have come to admit to myself that while I am aware I have some real difficulties with certain areas that smart people have dialed... on the whole: "Hey – eating Tide pods is not smart-o'meter... I'm killing it. That's not going to even be in the top 1000 of 'things I need to be advised on,' and apparently, that makes me special. I had no idea! Well, actually there was this one time I knew I had to be pretty smart.

You see, I was watching the Super Bowl a few years ago, and the game was almost over, and Seattle was playing against that really pretty quarterback... (he who must not be named.) The clock was nearing zero and Seattle was on, like, the 2-yard line with four downs available. Four downs! Four chances to get the ball a few inches in front of them and win the Superbowl. And they decided to throw... an interception. Of course, an interception, because they weren't playing against a freshman football team, they were playing the best team in the United States of Football!! And of course, the Patriots are more than capable of getting an interception when they only have to cover a couple dozen square feet with their entire defense. And as that Butler fella snatched the ball from the air to win that game, I thought...

"Huh, even I'm smart enough not to call THAT play."

A FAILED MOVIE

It was an awful movie, by anyone's measure. Truly awful. It was panned by critics; lost money. Almost no one bothered to see it. It won no awards (save some weird technical one for good snow...) and audiences did not like it. The public had been through some difficult days and were far too jaded for such a "happily ever after" film. The movie director lost his production company when the film failed and soon lost his career.

This is the fear we all have when we go out on a limb. Isn't it? When we dare to dream big? There is a lovely saying by Marianne Williamson that people often quote. She claims that our deepest fear is not that we aren't good enough, but that we are powerful beyond measure.

I'm calling male cow excrement on that one. (That's right – I said it.)

Do you actually believe that if you could be extraordinarily talented, intelligent or successful tomorrow, you'd shoot it down because you are afraid of being amazing? No – I don't think so. Every single lotto winner proves that you would take the upgrade. It may not be wise; there's certainly evidence that gain without sacrifice turns out poorly. But you aren't afraid of success. I don't see any actual evidence for that. So, what are you afraid of?

When the self-help book asks you to close your eyes and imagine what you would do if you could do anything in the world and then demands that you "Go do it now!!" why don't you? Well, I think you are afraid that you are incompetent. I am 100% sure that's what I am afraid of. You are afraid that your dream of being the next Bruno Mars is a poor choice to go steaming headlong after because you might not BE Bruno Mars. In fact – you may be the funny part of American Idol. The part where people try out for a singing show and between nerves and too many participation trophies seem unaware that they have no business singing on national TV. You may be brave enough to consider going after your dreams, but you are also wise enough to know that there is actually a good chance that you may not have the talent, or the time yet invested, (or the luck, or the connections) to achieve that dream.

But, here's the thing: the self-help book is right in saying you should go for things that you love... at least on some level.

I have debated (I'm still debating) regularly writing stories in this column about successful people and all of those folks who said they were terrible. We all know how many times JK Rowling was told Harry Potter was rubbish before it was published. I have no idea what a comedian like Adam Sandler was like as a child, but I am willing to bet his report cards don't say he was helpful and well-behaved. I bet his personality got shot down and belittled by a million frustrated adults. I bet he was the dream patient for every ADD drug company. No matter who I picture, every single success story from Lego's to Paperclips you know someone thought it was a waste of time... and I like telling those stories. The thing about trying something you really love is that you WILL fail along the way– often, and you have to be ok with that.

Accepting failure is probably the biggest secret to going for those big dreams. And, accepting failure is awkward and painful. But, you will be in the company of many amazing people who have plenty of failures themselves.

Remember that movie that failed? It truly was a disaster and really, if not for a small twist of fate would have stayed a complete flop (with good snow). But it's utter failure is likely the reason you've heard of it. Being such a complete loser, when the movie came up for copyright renewal - no one bothered. And so, with a festive holiday theme, and the fact that it now belonged to the public domain (which made it free), televisions stations began to show it at Christmas time. A whole new generation watched the movie for the first time and starting in the late 70's it became a holiday tradition.

This Christmas the odds are good that you too will sit down with your loved ones and revisit a young man as he fights with fate and failure. You will ache with him as the town of Bedford Falls brings him to the brink of suicide. But just as "It's a Wonderful Life" gave George Baily a reminder that failure is never final – the movie's director and producers found huge success with a whole new generation of American's who found the movie was the perfect Christmas tradition. Jimmy Stewart would go on to say that, in a career of amazing acting opportunities, playing George Baily was his favorite. And as a country of people who sometimes need a little courage to go for our big dreams, the movie is a reminder that a little failure isn't the worst thing ever. And everyone agrees, the snow was awesome.

SO DANG LOUD

It is so loud in my house right now. My fifteen-year-old is throwing a bottle on the hardwood floor over and over. And over. It's been going on forever.

My daughter is explaining to us that you make better decisions if you make them on a full bladder. I have heard this before; I believe it's true. The theory is being debated. The dog is growling and yipping. He is yipping at the empty Gatorade bottle that keeps smacking on the ground.

My husband just sneezed. So loud.

The debate on pee has ended. It has been determined that whatever the benefit to decision making, it comes at too great a cost to one's prostate. The girl has not mentioned that she is not a bearer of a prostate. That's a conversation for another day. The littlest girl has decided she wants to learn the guitar. She believes that picking up a toy guitar and wandering around singing the lyrics (incorrectly) to some Avett Brother's song constitutes a high level of competence. This is because her little friend had her first piano recital... so obviously this professional musician thing is immensely doable.

The dog is dizzy. This is true. The boy with the Gatorade bottle, deciding that he would no longer smack the floor with the bottle (this noise was deemed too loud) has moved on... so he and the dog are now wrestling. The dog is losing his mind. The noise has only gone up. But, the teenager has started spinning the doggie in circles. The dog is now stumbling around the house. It's hilarious. The coconut is a seed, not a legume. The girl found a new bit of data to share. The future height of the dog is also being discussed. There is concern that he will be too small. This is hilariously ironic. Everyone in this house is too small.

Sea otters have a million hairs on one square inch of their body.

The room finally stopped spinning for the dog. It just attacked the teenager. He didn't see it coming at all. I think the noise level may be coming down. Memories of awkward moments when the youngest commented on nuddie tudie bodies when observing "fine art" are being shared. Everyone is hysterical. It was pretty funny... a great sculpture loses something when a small child points out the awkward parts.

Tittle is the dot over an i. This fact has been debated and won by the teenager. Then the question is raised if the name is related to nipple? It got weird. The eleven-year-old is shouting about teats... I'm not sure how I feel about that. How have I lived forty years and I never heard about a tittle? Should I be concerned, or is it all right to have a child teaching me this now? I am confident that things are going to have to mellow soon. The Dad is finally getting tired of the noise. I can sense the tide turning. As long as I'm the only one overwhelmed the party will continue, but once I have a teammate, I will win the battle. (No one else is even aware that there is a battle... but I am slowly preparing.) An argument will soon be made that the pajamas and bedtime must commence. But not yet…

We are now debating the best phone voice mail announcements. We have agreed that a funny voicemail is annoying. It's only funny once. The boy stops spinning the dog and comments – he needs to update his, it's been the same for years. He made it before his voice had changed… I look to the father preparing for the cacophony to end – he must be annoyed – the little one is shrieking the wrong lyrics to a pop song that references putting someone's body on her… this is creepy -it's got to stop – my battle partner has arrived!

He is giggling and has the camera on the girl. This was not the response I needed. I can tell my in-laws will soon be receiving this video… The volume ratchets up.

It is so – very – loud - in my house right now.

HEALTHY HOLIDAY EATING

So I was informed that the theme for this month would be healthy holiday eating. Eating is fun...

Healthy eating... over the holidays?? Notsomuch.

But, I can address the subject I suppose. As a person with a decent BMI, I'll give you all my best advice for healthy eating. It's pretty simple: Salads.

What are you having for dinner tonight? No. Not that, you are having a salad. Tomorrow for dinner? A salad.

What are you having for dinner on January 22, 2016? Yep. You are having a salad. You think I'm kidding... but I'm not. As an adult, you should live on salads, sometimes fruit with some yogurt. A little protein in the mix - but mostly lots and lots and lots of veggies. Tons of salad.

Why so much salad? Because you are not sixteen. You do not have the metabolism of a sixteen-year-old - a metabolism that is driving you to destroy the Saxons, conquer foreign lands and spread your... fertileness.

No - you are a grown up.

You pay taxes and floss and use your turn signal before you change lanes. You show up on time to work and you don't honk and throw a tantrum every time you feel irritated in traffic. You swallow your frustrations, you wipe little one's dirty faces and pick up other people's smelly socks. You organize, you fix and you eat salads.

Because a healthy, functioning adult generally has a metabolism that could survive, just fine, on nothing but a cup of coffee and a tomato. Every day. Nothing else.

You aren't driven to conquer any more... you are now part of the maintenance crew. It may not sound glamorous, but it has its perks. Remember how desperate you once were to sit at the grownups table at Thanksgiving? Right? Remember how you wanted people to think your opinion mattered, but you were too young and inexperienced? Or what about wanting to make your own decision about what to buy, how to live, where to go? Boom. It's us! Maintenance Crew. We are the people who matter. We run the place, make the decisions, drive the economy. It's more mellow, sure, but it's actually a pretty cool gig.

So, personal opinion, I wouldn't worry about what you eat on Christmas. I wouldn't eat the sugar-free, low fat, made from tofu, pumpkin pie-fakie-whaties... I just wouldn't. If you are a real grownup, living a real healthy, salad filled grown-up life, then don't obsess over the extra calories in the wine, or the fat content in the gravy.

If you are a grown-up, and you are living well, then accept that your holidays are numbered. I am down to only seven Christmas's left with my oldest child at home. I am looking at the last few times he'll wake up Christmas morning as a member of this house. I'm not going to obsess about the fudge. Nope, I'm going to enjoy food, faith, family, friends. All the good "f-words." Because every other day I know I won't be eating fudge. I'll be eating salad.

I'll be driving kids to their important activities in their

important lives. I'll be cleaning bathtub drains, and finding lost homework. Sure, I have my own life, my own activities. But they aren't the "important ones." (I know you want them to be... but they kinda aren't... Nobody is coming to watch you play in your grown-ups softball league, although you are very cute hobbling around the bases with your dodgy knees.)

I think that – yes – we have joined the maintenance crew and left the days of war and pillaging behind us, but I'm actually digging the maintenance crew years.

Personally, I think salads are actually yummy. Grilled chicken on salad, grilled steak on salad, grilled shrimp on salad. Put enough meat and cheese on a salad and boom... not so bad.

And - maintenance crew – we are the world baby. We are the unsung heroes keeping this whole place running. And what those young folks out conquering haven't realized yet, is that we ARE the goal.

That lady with the salad in her hand, and a child on her lap, she's not yesterday's news; she's the monarch of the castle. Training up the warriors of the future, bringing hope and pumpkin pie to the masses. She has created a small kingdom in her home and here with her salad in hand, she rules her tiny empire along with the sexy guy with the dodgy knees. A small fiefdom ready to set the world ablaze with the mighty ideas... like: pick up your plate when you're finished, don't tease your sisters, be nice to people. And for crying out loud, when it's the holidays - just eat the fudge. You are a grown up. You eat your salads. It's time.

TAPE, TINSEL, AND TIMING THE PHOTOS...

I've learned that you can tell a lot about a man by the way he handles these three things: a rainy holiday, lost luggage, and tangled Christmas tree lights.

H. Jackson Brown, Jr. "Live and Learn and Pass It On"

I HAVE MASKING TAPE STUCK TO MY HEEL... FOR SURE. In my snow boot, of course, where I can't get to it, because we are at my child's school recital. She is playing something like a xylophone. My kid has her tongue stuck out at a weird angle. I think it's the cutest, but I know she's going to hate the photos. What is that thing she's playing? Is it a real instrument? She has been saying "tah tah tee tee tee tee tah" all stinking month – hopefully, this is the end of that. Pretty sure the song is Silent Night but it could be Jingle bells... it's hard to say.

Husband has to leave in five minutes because the Christmas pageant for church has rehearsal tonight and two of our kids are in that thing. We have three dance performances, three school parties, two work parties, a neighborhood party, gymnastics, and wrestling will have Christmas parties, three of my friends are having, in order: an ornament exchange, a cookie exchange, and a white elephant exchange. I have to go to Fabula and get some exchangeable stuff! And I have no party clothes... well, none that fit right now. Stupid eggnog. Sheshe stop is needed as well. Next week is a dress rehearsal and extra practice. Don't forget extra food for the food drives. I have already purchased the gifts for my side of the family, but not his. I wish postage didn't cost so much. Who am I kidding? I'm mailing them all Enstrom's again. It never fails. I will never actually give anyone a thoughtful gift for the rest of my life. It's too hard. Apparently, I just don't love them enough.

I haven't gotten his gift yet either. Why are men so difficult to buy for? Seriously. Men. If they want it, they own it —unless it costs a bajillion dollars; then there's a reason they don't.

My husband is trying to take a photo of my daughter's tongue issue. The littlest one is antsy. She is pulling on the strings of a jacket in front of us. How long can I allow her to do this before I must stop pretending not to notice? I mean, yes – it's annoying. But, she will be much more annoying once I stop her.

The kids all have friends who gave them gifts. Didn't see that coming. I got nothing. Had a couple decks of cards stashed somewhere as a "just for in case" gift. Can't remember where they are stashed. Maybe behind the tangled Christmas lights that I keep ignoring in the basement (because, of course, I can't dispose of perfectly good Christmas lights... but I keep not putting them up because there's no amount of pretty worth the hassle.) They've been in a tangled bunch for almost a decade. Don't tell my husband... that sort of thing drives him insane. Fortunately, he never ever ventures into the area of the basement where the Christmas stuff is stashed. If you need to dispose of a body someday... I'm not saying it's a good idea to need such a thing – but my basement Christmas pile...? Perfect.

Dad grabs two kids and he's off. I think about the unwrapped Christmas gift in the back seat of the car. Too late – I can't holler at him in the middle of this. It's going to be an issue. Ugh! And I just remembered tomorrow I have extra kids for carpool. How am I going to get any cooking done if I spend three hours shuttling kids around this town! I need to get some pie dough made and stick it into the freezer, so it's ready next week. Christmas can't be next week! I still have to wrap gifts! And I keep forgetting to buy more tape. It needs to stop winding up on my socks instead of on the gifts! That's it. I'm setting the alarm on the phone. 'Don't forget to buy more tape!' Wait!!! Ahhh! Switch to video! She stopped doing that thing with her tongue.

LESSONS SCOTT TAUGHT

Scott was sick as a child. Very sick. He stopped growing and his parents anxiously went from doctor to doctor desperate to save their son. They were given a diagnosis - six months to live... but he lived through that. Then doctors thought cystic fibrosis... but that was wrong too. They tried different diets – but those made it worse. He was miserable, sick and would not grow. A doctor finally told his parents just to give up, and let him live his life. They didn't know what was wrong, or why, but all the diets and tests were cruel and unhelpful.

So, he got on with life. He also took up figure skating. With time he found he liked it, and he was pretty good; and with more time, he was great.

So great in fact, that he went to the Olympics, and it was there that Scott Hamilton won the gold. He was the best figure skater in the entire world, at 5′2 and 108 lbs. He was fun and unique. He could do a backflip on skates, he could launch into jumps and twists better than any other person alive. And he could do it so well, in large part, because he was just so dang small! It's always been true that certain sports, like gymnastics – or figure skating, just work better for tiny bodies. His was tiny, and he used every inch he lacked to his advantage.

Later, when his amateur career was over, and his life was focused as a sports commentator and performer he discovered that he had cancer. In fact – he'd always had cancer. A congenital growth on his pituitary gland that had been the cause of the stunted growth all along. It was dangerous, and it was killing him. It was also what made him great.

We live in an age where we are learning to "fix" ourselves. Even if you aren't an aluminum foil hat wearing conspiracist, the work being done in China with CRISPR technology modifying human DNA should give you pause.

We may soon be able to weed out our "flaws." That's the plan anyway. A recent news program on CBS lauded that Downs Syndrome has been cured in Iceland... just kidding... it hasn't been cured... it has been eradicated – by killing those who have the condition. This is being heralded with the same arguments the eugenicists of the 1930's dreamed up. We can weed out the weak, frail, ugly and help evolution to create a world of our "best." Perhaps Scott Hamilton can step into this discussion much as Jesse Owens did in the 1936 Olympics. A reminder that what the world shuns is often the best and brightest we have. That the things that make us different, or broken, are the things that can make us great. We are so quick to embrace "normal." Normal isn't our best; it isn't our boldest or most valuable. When we fix the flaws, we lose the brilliance. From kids with attention deficit disorders, or Asperger's, or even cancer, how often do we lose the very thing that would have made them unique or amazing in an effort to 'fix' their flaws?

We aren't all meant to be 5'10, or sit still, or socialize easily. We are weird, loud, shy, lumpy, odd... and even sick. And I'd sure appreciate it if we'd start celebrating the broken, at least a little. I am thrilled that a full grown man can weigh only 108 lbs and use that unique build to rock the world with his talent. As William Arthur Ward once said: "Adversity causes some men to break; others – to break records."

A PILGRIMAGE AND TURNING 40

I know that most people read this column to get a dose of humor. A quick injection of thoughts on the bizarre, or unusual or just plain weird. And, I am generally happy to oblige. (Truth be told, I'm not much good at writing anything else.) This is why I am a bit concerned that I won't start Friday morning with my regular, "LOL texts" from local friends with their thoughts on the latest column (looking at you Rick LaPena.) But, I'm afraid I'm in a bit of an unusual writing space, and I believe I'd like to pass my bittersweet thoughts along.

I will be spending my fortieth birthday in Israel. I have always wanted to go, and visit the birthplace of my faith; to see the lauded fertile crescent and stand in the place of legends. Stand where Moses stood, walk where David walked, learn where Deborah learned. These are stories from my childhood, and stories that shaped the values of nations. Stories that changed the course of history, beliefs that conquered the world. It's impossible to overstate the significance of these stories and the very real people and places that they came from. Anthropologists may disagree on who existed, or when they existed – or even if they existed. But, the best ideas were born here, and whatever is historical fact and whatever is embellished legend – it was birthed in this little tiny corner of the planet. A ridiculously, insignificant chunk of land. It's not as pretty or as productive as most any other place on earth. It's not wealthy in any great commodity. The one commodity it can lay claim to? Stories. Really important stories. Stories that became ideas. Ideas that became movements. Movements that changed the world.

I was a flight attendant in my early 20's and I spent my time very independently and I loved it. That all changed one January afternoon when a medical tech with weird makeup told me the test said I was pregnant. From that day forward, I have made every single decision based on the needs and wishes of others. What they want to do, when they need to eat, or go to the bathroom or take a nap? I have four people in my life who's wishes matter more to me than do my own. What are their interests? Their passions? Their goals, dreams, ideas? This is what I care about.

It didn't happen overnight... but gradually – through 9 months of growing a baby within... and a bit of that first year. Somewhere – my priorities just shifted. But this adventure will be just for me. I'm going to Israel alone. Solo mìo. I am making a bit of a pilgrimage of it. I am taking something from my father and my mother (both of whom died far too young,) and I am bringing those tokens with me. I plan to leave them in Israel.

I won't be focused on the passions of my husband or the needs of my kids. Just me – being me. To be very honest, I'm scared... Every time I start to get excited, I read another reason to worry about the violence and animosity between the people who share that stretch of dirt. It means so much to them—and no one is willing to give an inch in claiming land they absolutely believe belongs to them. It seems silly to those of us who have no strong connection to the land we live in. (Just stick a price on it and let the free market sort it out – 'Merica!) But, I believe the Native Utes of this area could explain to us, just how painful losing the land of your ancestors can be, and why people would passionately and violently defend it... and of course... both feel justified.

I am also sad. I want in so many ways to share my adventure with the people I love. I don't want to have a magical moment all alone. I don't want to step foot in the Sea of Galilee and not share it with... anyone -at all.

But, I do desperately want to remember what it feels like to live my own plans and my own dreams. To remember the me I am, deep down, when no one else requires my attention. The decision to make raising my children my utmost priority is something I will never regret. Jaqueline Kennedy once said, "If you bungle raising your children, I don't think whatever else you do matters very much." I am desperate not to bugle it. I am determined with every ounce within me, that I will do this one thing well. (I sure hope I will.) I will raise and tend to and love and scold and grow these children to be kind, good, brave, strong people who make the world a better place. Period. That is my only goal. It has been my only guiding principle for almost 16 years. But, for this one week, I am going to be just me. Following the roads that mean so much to me, the ideas that rocked my world, changed my heart – focused my priorities. And this is a part of mothering. The part where you let go and evolve out of the raising. This is the beginning of a change.

I will become more of a mentor – less of a parent. I hate losing their dependence on me. It has given me such meaning and value. I matter because they matter. This means I will have to begin a life of meaning and purpose independent of their needs. I can't fathom it, and it isn't fully here yet. I am not an empty nester – that's more than a decade away, but we are walking that direction. My oldest starts driving this year. The tight, safe, firm, grip I held on him is loosening up. I hate it and love it in the same breath. The world that was born the day the tech said a test was positive is coming to its end. And as the pain and beauty of all of this whirls around me – I will head out on this mini-pilgrimage. I will visit the holy, sanctified, set aside, places of the world. Places where the best of us died for ideas. I am so scared and so excited. It's the precipice—of whatever comes next.

RECIPE FOR DISASTER

Einstein once said that everyone is a genius, but if you judge a fish on his ability to climb a tree, he will spend his life believing he is stupid. I can seem deceptively intelligent. Schools focus on issues like reading and math- areas that I have always been rather competent. I was always an above average student, because no teacher gave a test on organization, or remembering where you put your keys, or which day of the week it is. The truth is, in the real world, where practical skills matter, I am often on the low end of the curve. And every now and then, there are going to be consequences.

Recipe For Disaster:

Ingredients:

1 c. Hubris, 1 Tbs. Assumptions, 1 tsp. Mistakes, 3 cups (give or take) Failed Backup Plans, a dash of Utter Despair

Directions:

1. We will start with a generous cup of **Hubris**. This is how our adventure begins... "Twyla," our leading lady says to herself, "You can totally take this trip alone! There are

millions of people in Israel functioning day in and day out with no problems, yes you have a language issue, and yes you don't know a lick about life there, but if millions of people are functioning there just fine, then I'm sure you can figure it out." And so, with a wing and a prayer our heroine lands in the Holy Land, grabs a rental car and is off to Jerusalem. No big thing! Upon arriving it appears that parking is going to be a bit of an issue, but she has already googled a parking structure near the Jaffa Gate – (her destination) when it turns out her preferred parking lot is full - a quick drive just a few blocks away reveals another lot. That Jerusalem is entirely one color (beige) and the streets all look identical does not concern our protagonist and she proceeds to wander into the Old City with no need to return to her rental car for 3 days.

2. Add one tablespoon **Assumptions**. Our heroine may have assumed that as long as she is within a few blocks of her original Google Maps parking structure (for which she retains an address) she will have no problem finding her new lot. One must assume that she will totally remember what she was thinking three days ago. One must also assume she will be able to recognize one beige building from the next when she already is ridiculously inobservant. One must again assume that she's, well... competent.

3. Now we need to fold in a teaspoon of **Mistakes**. Not a big mistake... just a, "I need to clean out these old receipts from my bag." So, a quick clean up means the receipt for the parking structure is tossed. A little mistake... that will prove large in the near future.

4. Here we are going to need to add a large cup of **Failure on the Backup Plan**. A wizened woman traveling abroad may become heavily dependent on Google

Maps. She may then be dismayed when her Google Maps app is being a bit wonky and hopping around a bit when trying to locate recent locations... she may then struggle to load backup data clarifying where she may have wandered just a few short days ago.

5. Another cup of **#4**. She may then try the backup plan of contacting her credit card company. After all, they will have the address of where she purchased her parking space. But her credit card company will prove to be closed. Ummm... CLOSED? This is TRUE!!!!! When this internationally ginormous credit card company's number was called there was only a recorded message saying they were busy and to call back in 4 hours. No human being was available... no information available... nothing. On the back of said credit card it says, "24-hour customer support." That's a big, fat, lie. It's: "24-hour customer support...until the morning you might be lost in Jerusalem all by yourself and really need the address for the place you purchased parking three days ago... then we are busy." No one will even answer the phone. Just... nothing. (I would hate to disparage anyone in this public forum but let's say our leading ladies card was a Shmaster Shmard... a shmaster shmard from shmiddy bank. She may have then found herself calling... and walking... and calling... and walking... for 5 hours.

6. Another cup of **#4**. Our girl has another brilliant idea. What about her rental car company? Perhaps they have GPS on the car and can locate it? No. No, they cannot.

A DASH OF **UTTER DESPAIR**: So she called her husband. In Montrose. In the middle of the night... And cried a little bit. He was very sleepy, very kind, and a bit confused. He did remind her that he really couldn't do much... what with the Atlantic between them...

Finally, complete the recipe with a big splash of a **Hail Mary Pass**... begging.

What could be more appropriate than pulling a Hail Mary Pass in the Holy Land, right? Our protagonist began to beg for help from everyone. She pleaded for help from the men in parking structures, from women in business attire, and from rental car agency. Everyone was very kind and made a sincere effort to help. Really, everyone. But, the car rental agency, Enterprise, did even more. They hired a driver to come out and drive her around looking for her car. Mr. Moti, our tale's knight in shining armor, drove her around - for hours. Our duo would quickly bond over local politics, pictures of their children, and the valiant search for her car. Eventually, there was a miracle... or more precisely, Google Maps finally got a decent signal and sure enough, our lady traced back her locations to the day she had parked and right there in her Google Maps history was the exact address. When she had parked, "a few blocks away" from her original parking structure it was actually miles away.

This recipe for disaster baked up into quite a mess. It was a long, hot, sweaty, miserable day and I was so frustrated with myself and a bit with my credit card. But, the flip side was that I got a new friend, and a much better sense of the city of Jerusalem, their streets, people and politics. It was actually the day that I learned the most; the day I got to really meet the people and explore the city. And Mr. Moti not only would assure me when I grew tired, that the rental car company told him to help me for as long as it took; he also kept reminding me that it's just a car. And I often need to remember not to get upset about things that aren't important. Because what really matters is not the well-baked disaster that I was living through that day, my true valuables were tucked away on the other side of the world -sleeping the night away.

THE SINNERS AND THE SAINTS

Have you ever really listened to the voice in your head? I know some of ya'll think in images, but I think in words... conversations – (there are a few going all the time actually.) I'm not crazy. Pretty sure. They have tests.

But, unless it's 3 a.m. I'm not interested in the conversations in my head. (I read a joke recently online... it went as so: My brain at 3 a.m. "The bills! My responsibilities! What is the meaning of life??" My brain at 3 p.m. "Potato, potato... ching-chong tomato."

That's my reality. If it's 3 am the conversations in my head are quite anxiety-inducing and obnoxious. The rest of the time they're just a bit of background noise. However, in Israel, I found my mind was quite distracting, and often... highly inappropriate.

This was most obvious when I was in very holy places. I'm talking...like- very holy. Like the place Jesus was crucified. That's a big deal. Especially after you leave your kids and husband and spend money you really can't afford to spend and take time off of work you probably shouldn't take and make all of these sacrifices largely in order to make a spiritual pilgrimage to one of the holiest places on earth! So, it would be terrible, should you find yourself in the holiest possible place to think something you shouldn't! It would be downright shameful, in fact, if you were to say... find yourself dripping with sweat, crowded and miserable and thinking... "Ugh, this is heck." (But your naughty brain said a different word at the end.)

I KNOW!!!!! It's the WORST!!! But, you don't think about what you should think!! You don't think about what NOT to think! Thoughts just pop into your head! It is awful. Really, really, horrible to find that particular thought popping into your head at that particular time. But it DID! With no one to talk to, nothing around to distract me I stood in a very crowded obnoxious line of fellow Christian pilgrims with people pushing to slowly move towards two holy spots (the place Jesus was crucified and buried.)

The folks running the Church of the Holy Sepulcher really need to have a quick chat with the folks at Disney. Not just because they could have a conversation on staging and thematic mood... which they could. But, more importantly, line management is really lacking. It's basically a free for all of people pressing towards the two holy locations and shoving their way closer to the front.

This disorganized hot, stuffy, chaotic, environment makes for a myriad of thoughts and emotions... none of them really what you would call pious, religious, holy, or meaningful. No beautiful emotion was naturally bubbling to the forefront. But irritations, selfishness, anger... those emotions were in full bloom. One could argue it was a great opportunity to test my self-control, to find my true, shallow, self-absorbed, sinner and slap her around a bit.

Truth is... that thought... 'ugh this is heck;' that thought bubbled up... repeatedly. At well over 90 degrees, high humidity, people shoving me, a scarf on my head that I'm not used to (and might feel offended by...?) it was not my happy place.

Then I arrived at the final location! I was going to walk into an inner sanctum. (A holy building inside of The holy building.) I needed to hurry. I knew how hot and miserable the people behind me felt, and I knew I should just check it out and move on. Then something happened. I don't know how, or why but suddenly everyone pushed forward. I was crammed in front of a group of German tourists and they were all pressing against me... and a German lady in her 60's had her hand... on my behind. I don't know if you've dealt with such harassment in your life? When you are young and this happens, you feel embarrassed or ashamed and you do nothing. Somewhere around 18, you get some confidence and then someone gets slapped. I am now 40. I'm well into the 'slap people who grab my behind' phase. I need you to picture this moment. I am about to visit the tomb that the body of Christ was most likely buried in... the place I believe he was resurrected... a place I never thought I would actually visit in my entire life. And it's really happening. And I'm fighting off the miserable heat, humidity and naughty thoughts comparing my discomfort to h.e. double hockey sticks. And having arrived at the entrance of the site, a woman's hand is firmly pressing into my rear end! (In her defense, I believe she was trying to grip her purse and has her hand stuck now that the crowd is shoving so hard). But here, in this second, about to visit such an important place, it takes everything in me to not turn around and smack her.

Well, my intense, impressive, self-control and the fact that I can't move anyway.

This was the experience I had when visiting many holy places. The Sea of Galilee was filthy, the place of the crucifixion and burial were crowded, hot, humid, miserable. The wailing wall had armed guards. And the old city was really awesome... but a lot like Tiajuana.

Isn't that the way a life of faith really is, though? It's almost never ethereal. You almost never see miracles. You rarely feel that moment where you genuinely believe that you and God are buddies. Most of my life, faith has been a mix of tortured logic, a daily practice akin to brushing my teeth, and a lot of messy, tedious, reality. But somehow... all that boring, ugly, pointless stuff becomes the most meaningful, profound part of my life.

In the place of saints... I was reminded - I'm a sinner.

However, just like in faith, every now and then, there is a moment.

I found a room. A small, boring, cold, dark room. I was all alone. A stranger led me to a church, a priest had explained a small plaque and I walked into that room as the only person in all of Israel who wanted to sit in that quiet place right then. The plaque described that the building had been excavated long ago and a small inscription was discovered in the wall going back to the third century. It stated that this home belonged to Mary... the mother of Mark... the author of a gospel. Her home is referred to in several passages as the upper room. I knew exactly where I was, and I knew exactly why this place mattered.

And all alone, in the dark, cold room. I listened as a woman sang to herself in Aramaic, the language Jesus; the language of the original Jews and Palestinians of the first church. I stood in the very spot that the original church was formed – the place where it all began. I cried - a little. And I didn't have grumpy, bitter thoughts, and I didn't want to hit anyone. For just a minute, I wasn't just a sinner... I was in the presence of saints.... For a moment I held a tiny miracle.

ISRAEL FINAL INSTALLMENT

The plane was making a really weird noise. A weewahh-weewahh... it made me nervous. I know a plane can be more than solid and yet look and sound a bit janky. Still, I wasn't looking forward to a 4-hour flight with that noise.

Then the pilot came on overhead. He said there was a technical issue and we were returning to the airport. My first thought was irritation... I was going to get stuck over here and miss my daughter's birthday and she would never forgive me. But then another thought took its place. I was going to return to Israel?? At the height of their Holy Days?? Because something was wrong with my plane?

Suddenly my mind started thinking much scarier thoughts. Thoughts about ways a terrorist might make a statement using the plane I was sitting in. The landing gear came down. That was a relief, but then the runway came into view. There were fire engines, police cars, and ambulances EVERYWHERE. Why on earth do they need all of this stuff? Suddenly I was terrified. But it was only another minute and we were on the ground. Whew!!! So we are fine

– obviously... except they are not getting us off. It was another 5 minutes of watching Paramedics watching you. Wishing someone would tell you if you needed to worry.

Only upon walking off of the plane as flight attendants in emergency vests helped us did we find out that we had lost an engine – likely to a bird strike. No terror attack – most of the time I'd been worried I was actually over the dangerous part.

That nerve-wracking flight had begun with an overnight at the airport in Tel Aviv because security takes forever, upon landing I spent hours getting back out of security the wrong way – then back into line to find a new way to the US – sent to a new airline that almost closed before I finally persuaded them to let me please get a flight. Then a mad rush through a million layers of security followed by a 13-hour flight – and 3-hour layover, a 5-hour flight a trip to find my car and a 5-hour drive home to Montrose – and of course, I got pulled over around Glenwood for a headlight.

I arrived home at 3 am the morning of my daughter's birthday – and threw up. I have decided I don't need to go anywhere – ever. You know where you can go to see immense beauty? Right here. Do you know where you can find amazing food and awesome people? Right here. You know where you can go to hike and climb and raft, and ski. Or if you're like me—sit in a hot spring while your friends do that stuff? Right here!

I'm not saying that travel isn't important, or that I don't think it's good for our minds to experience other cultures, beliefs, traditions, and social cues. It's good—it's an important part of a balanced education. But, for right now—I'm over it. I get to wake up every day in (I honestly believe) one of the greatest places on the planet. I think I'll just hang out here for a while.

DEFENDING THE GIRLS

I HAVE A DAUGHTER, I HAVE TWO ACTUALLY. THERE IS something difficult about raising a girl, especially in our extra unique world. Can we all just admit that life today is nothing at all like life years ago and in certain ways it's disproportionately hurting my girls? I once saw my son and daughter playing when they were just little bitty. My son had a pretend bow and arrow, my daughter was hauling around a baby doll and they were on some imagined adventure. I remember thinking how quintessentially human that moment was. Pick any little boy and girl a thousand years ago, just playing around, and the odds that the boy would be running around with a pretend bow and arrow and his sister would be hauling her baby doll seems very high. There is something inherent in this longing for almost all kids through all of history, and it was true with mine. My son had stuffed animals and baby dolls they were for wars and target practice. Make no mistake, he still may give a stuffed teddy a snuggle... after he had killed it a few times first.

My daughters love hunting, they are tough and determined and they sports and wrestling with their brother, but the first time my daughter saw a baby doll she picked it up and cradled it in a way my son had never done. I hadn't even thought of buying her one until she saw her first and it was the best thing EVER!! So here I am raising such quintessentially traditional kids but this is not a quintessentially traditional world. And I'm of two minds about that.

Part of me is like. Good riddance to bad rubbish. The "traditional" world hosed women, and I'm never going back. I like voting... and I'm downright brilliant—obviously. (I mean, I think you all should be privy to my thoughts every other week... so I must assume I'm worth it.) And, I'll be danged if any man will say that he should be teaching me and not the other way around, not because he knows more, but because he can't bear children. No – I'm all for equality and I've got no interest in going backward.

But, I also have daughters and I'll admit we are different. When I'm at work... I don't want more money for more hours... I want flex time and work from home opportunities. I want my girls to be free to like pink or babies or weird eyebrows just because they're trendy. (Did you know weird eyebrows are a thing??) Hey, teenage girls doing the weird eyebrows. When I was young—girls were shaving the eyebrows off and then drawing them on and then they'd draw black around their lips... not on their lips... around. Take it from me, going trendy with your face is a bad idea. It's a bad idea to be too trendy with your clothes... but it's a terrible idea with your face!!! But, this brings me to a real fear I have: our daughters are being damaged by new trends, and I need to fight for them, just as my grandmother's and mother's generations fought for me.

All of my kids are athletic—one of my daughters is a pretty awesome sprinter. The fifth-grade track and field meet made it pretty clear, she has a future in sprinting should she choose and the fates allow. But—these days Title Nine does not protect her opportunity to compete as a girl. These days a boy who has been born with a whole slew of physical benefits she will never get can take away her chance to compete. It's happening, and it happens more every year.

A generation of girls who would hold state records are losing those records to biological boys competing as the gender they identify with, not the biological advantage they are born with. A generation of girls is losing first place in high school state competitions, or a chance to podium at state, or even to have made it to a state competition because a biological boy took that position. Women are once again being taken advantage of by men based on a man's vision of himself, and his choice – the girls get no choice in that. Just the loss of opportunity.

I'm not ok with it. I'm really not. I look at my daughter and the female athletes of her generation and I hate watching them disabused of their opportunities and I'm determined to defend them. This cannot last for long or Title 9 and all that it accomplished will be ruined. There will only exist sports for males.. Males competing as men and class b for males competing as women. Are the women losing their state titles or state records as high school athletes getting an astrix? (This record is held female who was born male... – the record for the biological female stands at ...?) A Pandora's box has been opened by our generation based on the completely intangible, immeasurable, unscientifically definable support for a person's life experience. And my daughters and their friends will be losing athletic opportunities because of this. I think it should be straightforward... if you will never train, or compete, while experiencing menstrual cramping, then you are not on a level playing field and should not be given the awards for that event. And if it bothers you to imagine that menstruation is an element that female athletes face, I promise you, the experience of a biological female is not even touched on with that one component. Pregnancy scares, birth control effects, the physical limitations of breasts, or hips, or ovulation pain or having to halt your career for pregnancy, or childbirth, or breastfeeding. A twenty-year-old female athlete is facing a myriad of needs, experiences and choices a biological male regardless of his gender identity will never be subjected to. These statements should go without saying. This shouldn't need to be voiced. My daughter's opportunities should never be affected by a person who won't know these realities regardless of that person's personal life experience.

A decade ago she wanted to hold the baby-doll and that was just the beginning of my acceptance that her world was different, and unique and deserved respect and defense against those who would try to hold her back. I will fight for her, and the female athletes that deserve the protections Title 9 fought for, long before they could have imagined they would need this defense.

BULLETS AND BAD IDEAS

I'm going to tell you a story: You are sitting on the couch with your significant people. They call it Netflix and chill these days... I think... unless that means something else... (which it might). But, in my scenario, you are actually chilling and actually watching a movie on Netflix. The music gets dramatic – and the good guy gets shot!

Wow! Now the music is threatening! Everyone is rushing and terrified. He's dying! Oh no! We have to get the bullet out! They scramble. They dig around. Sometimes it's so threatening, so dangerous – we got to just get in there with our bare hands! The music is reaching a fevered pitch!!!! They got the bullet! Glory be! He is saved! The bullet is gone and the music turns to joy. The good guy kisses the pretty girl... she cries a bit. And it's time to begin the happily ever after montage. Great flick.

This scene is SO common... I have watched it a million zillion times, and so have you. And do you know what every single hunter or ER nurse or trauma surgeon in the world is saying as they watch??

"You do NOT need to get the bullet out!!!!"

WHY? Is it a bomb-bullet? Is it going to explode? What idiot created the, "We gotta get the bullet out!" scenario and why has no one EVER explained that there is nothing that will magically kill the person by leaving the bullet? And conversely, taking the bullet out doesn't magically save them! This cannot be rocket science here. Cut the green wire on the bomb... take the bullet out of the shoulder... same thing.

No. No, it's not. You can live the rest of your life with a bullet in you – plenty of people do. It's the HOLE that is deadly – and digging around in the HOLE is only MORE deadly!!

I wonder how many people have died because the first person on a scene started digging around in a bullet hole because they saw it on TV??

"Well Jim, the coroner says our boy would have survived, but Susie Jane arrived on scene and was determined to save him. She knew from decades of television that she had to get the bullet out to save his life! So the wound that had avoided major organs and was beginning to clot and heal was instead torn apart by Susie's well-intentioned digging and he bled out. She killed him with her helpfulness."

Never, never, ever, ever has there been an imminent threat posed by a bullet. There is a threat from the hole the bullet tore into the person. But there is nothing the bullet is doing inside of the body that means it cannot just sit there... indefinitely really. Certainly – nothing that removing it suddenly fixes. If the bullet WAS a danger, it would likely be because it was sitting a hair away from severing an artery or something, which would make removing the bullet a priority – but – not in a movie way.

Imagine that dramatic music! We need to remove the

bullet! It is dangerously close to an artery! So first there's the slow, careful transportation. Prepping, anesthesia, taping up and sterilizing followed by a cautious surgery. Intense, scary music drones on and on as the surgeon ask the tech, "So, how was your daughter's field trip yesterday?"

Now, I know, this is just one of a million obnoxious things we watch that we all know are ridiculous. Let's add to the list:

Swat teams running into the big scary drug bust scene dressed in sexy outfits and un-sensible shoes. EVERY TIME! There's a bunch of "regular" swat team guys who show up dressed appropriately, (like people who don't want to die,) and then the actors who, for some reason, never change out of the high heels, fitted suits and slippy shoes. Their bulletproof vests are never covering enough to make them look bulky, they always somehow look like they belong in the matrix, not on an actual cop.

Or, the cute leading lady who looks like she's never eaten her salad with dressing magically flipping 250-pound giant men over her back by twisting their arms just right. It NEVER looks, at all, like the man just threw himself over her back and landed moaning. (That last part was sarcasm... for those of you in Rio-Linda.)

What about those white guys in the Star Wars movies? I believe they are called storm troopers. What does that white plastic armor even do? I'm serious! They die constantly. Ants are harder to kill than those guys. And, while I'm complaining, why when there is a big fight scene, with 8 bad guys to 1 good guy, do all the bad guys take turns? This is obviously a huge advantage for the good guy. Then it's just a question of the good guys' endurance... which is generally exceptional in movies. You'd think it would occur to them to just tackle him all at once. But, it never does.

They learned to take turns in grade school, and now it is to the good guys' advantage. Bad guys love to follow the rules.

Now, let me admit. This column is obnoxiously snarky, and generally, I hate that person who ruins a good movie for you by pointing out all the ways it violates the laws of physics or reminding you that the plot line has some glaring hole. Leave it; it's supposed to be entertaining. It's fiction.

I'm generally a big fan of crashes, and crazy suspense, and a wild plot. I really am. So, I hate to be the nit-picky punk that is ruining a great movie by pointing out this stuff. But, just today, I was listening to an expert; a genuinely smart historian, explaining that the Archduke Franz Ferdinand of Austria likely died, in part, because he was so wealthy they often sewed him into his clothes. This was tragic because it kept them (sigh*) from removing the bullet in time.

This is true. I'm not joking. An actual person, who I am certain has far more degrees, with capital letters following his name, and has read far more books than I have… believes that life or death can be skirted, by the ability to remove a bullet in time.

So obviously, I HAD to write about it. It could save a life.

THE INVENTOR OF THE HIGH FIVE COULD ONLY HIGH FOUR... AND POLITICS

So, the guy who invented the high five... He could only high four. This is true. He was missing his thumb. The thumb-less athlete was a basketball player named Wiley Brown. Brown managed to be a tremendous athlete despite the amputated thumb, and he often would "low five...-four" his teammate Derek Smith. Low fiving was a very common thing back in the seventies, having been invented in the twenties by 'beatniks' and 'jazz aficionados' (they were the hula hooping Telluride hippies of their day). So, by the seventies, low fives had been around for decades. They were super common. Everyone was low fiving everywhere... but something was missing. You could sense the despair, palpable, across sports arenas worldwide. Basketball players were often to be seen yawning as they gave their low impotent fives. But then– on a brilliant evening, while practicing basketball in 1979 for their University of Louisville, national championship season, everything changed. Smith dropped his outstretched hand to inspire a low five from Brown who responded with a look... a pause... and then Brown said, "No, up high." And then our four-fingered friend and his buddy, for the very first time in history, threw their hands up... and did a high five/four!

Unless they didn't. I mean they say they did... but then there's this other story, about some other guys, who may have done it two years earlier. Baseball players. Glen Burk of the Dodgers is said to have thrown his hand up in exuberation at home plate and his teammate Dusty Baker, not knowing just what to do, jumped up and hit it. They claim this practice continued, and a few years later they even had high-fiving shirts made.

What to do, what to do??

The politics of the great high fiving debate has become heated. (Not just a narrative choice to suit my story.) Those basketball fans cannot allow the glorious low five to high five moment to be tarnished by a bunch of baseball players! And, the baseball players are sick of the basketball players stealing their glory! But, the basketball players have a video of their team constantly high fiving that fateful year. Empirical evidence that high fiving took off once they started. No one has a video of the baseball claim. Although baseball players point out - that's simply because baseball is a boring sport. So why would you video it? (Baseball fans are notoriously super-laid-back when you make fun of their sport... super chill.)

So, now we are at an impasse. The stakes could not possibly be higher. The fate of high fiving lies in the balance, and no one will give. But then, a twist!

The Beatniks are livid! Apparently, some people still read poetry? (And you thought baseball was boring!) It turns out, the poets want their low five back and are tired of athletes appropriating their culture. How will this end?

Who will win? Why did that guy not have a thumb? In the politics of high fiving... the story is far from finished!

Have thoughts or passionate opinions on this subject? Please contact me at Twyladoesntreadthis@nomail.com. I will totally read it.

BOREDOM

"I'm sorry I smacked you, I was afraid you'd never stop talking, and I panicked!"
Author Unknown

I'M NOT ALWAYS THE MOST EXCITING PERSON. Sometimes when I'm talking to my children, telling them the secrets of the universe... explaining profound - truly profound truths - that will forever alter the way they see the world, their eyes glaze over a bit. You know the look? And I notice that while they may physically still be in the same room with me, they have taken their soul to some other locale where they could avoid me and my profound truths.

It may totally shock you to hear my husband does this as well. In fact, that man has it down to an art. He's a dang expert at fake listening. Honestly; he could teach a class. He has learned to not only do the murmurs that he obligatorily will pepper into my story: "Mmmmm.... Uh-huh.... Mmmmmm.... Yeah?" He also has developed higher level zone-out skills. Here's the real trick. When he has reached peak boredom and I am finally acknowledging that his brain is doing something far more interesting than listening to me... like re-organizing his socks by color in his head; I call him out!!!!

I say, "Hey! You're not even listening to me!!!" And he can then, without fail, recite the last ten words I said.

"Sure I am," he argues, "You said: ...The guy in front of me in the line wanted cheese."

Now, what do I do? I know he wasn't listening. I know he has just developed the married ninja skills of: 'repeat back the last thing your wife said.' But can I ever prove that? No. He's got it nailed!

But the truth is, boredom is a problem for all people, not just those who live with me. As rather spoiled Americans we are exceptionally prone to the issue.

Boredom is actually form of torture. In fact, it may be the most effective form. That is why isolation is the form of punishment that prisons use as their "big guns." I know, it doesn't make sense, pain should be the ultimate torture, right? In fact, every single parent of a toddler is calling bull-poopy on that idea. They'd give their right arm for a moment of peace and quiet. They are hiding in the shower right now, just for a chance to get a break from the crazy life with a little tiny person hell-bent on dying every other second.

But, even for those of you with toddlers... apparently, boredom is the worst kind of torture.

You doubt me? You'd like some evidence? Well, dear reader, I got you.

The University of Virginia did a study in which they took people and stuck them in a room with nothing to do for 15 minutes and watched them devolve into desperate misery. This wasn't one person, it was everyone. No one decided to go zen and meditate, and for the record, napping wasn't allowed. After discovering that the total lack of self-control or imagination necessary in order to sit for 15 minutes was almost universal, the professors decided to 'up the anti.' They put an interesting option in the room with these people. A machine to deliver painful electric shocks. They just left it in the room with these people who had nothing to do for 15 minutes to see if they'd shock themselves. AND THEY DID!!!! The typical American if forced to choose between 15 minutes of boredom and physical pain WILL PICK PAIN!!!!! How crazy is that? Be honest... would you do it? I almost immediately thought I would. I am busy enough as a mom to believe that 15 minutes in a room alone actually sounds pretty awesome, but I am curious enough that a part of me kinda believes that I'd be shocking myself in no time.

All evidence suggests that my family pretty regularly thinks an electric shock would be an antidote to my voice as well. Now, you may believe that their lack of enthusiasm in hearing me discuss the thrilling day I had: scanning documents, hustling the carpool, making spaghetti pie... living the dream... hurts my feelings. But actually, I am comfortable with the knowledge that I bring about a sliver of boredom into their lives. I think I've earned the torture after surviving their toddler years. Plus, I have learned a few tricks as well, I may not have the ninja 'repeat the last ten words back to you' deal... but I have my own discovery.

You touch them on the nose.

I'm not saying it makes me interesting, but I have found that people suddenly pay attention. The risk here is that you may get whacked. It turns out touching some people on the nose elicits an impulse to touch your face back, quickly, with their hand in a fist, and with force. But, this does allow you to hone your reflexes and, I promise, they're not bored.

MOMMY THE MINI-VAN

I wonder if I have become my mini-van? I always laughed when people cared all that much about the car they were driving—especially what it looks like. "It's just a car! It performs a function," says I, "It gets you from here to there." I could care less what it looks like; I want it to be able to perform that function well. That meant going fast when I was young, chronically late and living in Los Angeles. Good in the snow, and a manual for easy passing when I was even younger, learning to drive back roads of Delta County. But now I'm a Mom and multiple cup holders, the ability to clean, (and to hide what's not clean), for kids to avoid touching one another, and the sliding doors that keep kids from dinging the cars near us upon entry and exit... those are my priorities now. (You're welcome people of Montrose).

But today, I cannot help but wonder if my lack of interest in a cool, sexy car doesn't begin to emulate a lack of interest in cool, sexy... well, anything. I was cool in my twenties... and sexy for sure. Ok... truthfully, I may not have been cool. I was in the university choir, and we did use jazz hands and a whole lot of highly unnecessary smiling. Like WAY too much smiling. The kind where you need to look somewhere else because the all-girl choir in their bright fuschia pink dresses won't stop staring right at you and smiling. With jazz hands. (I may not have been cool.)

I was definitely sexy, though. I mean – you have to give me this one. Here's my evidence: I was a female... in my twenties. I think that clears it up. Of course, when you are a female in your twenties, you don't THINK you're sexy. You think you're lumpy and dimply and weird. But, twenty is when the bloom is on the rose. Twenty is your body in its full perfection doing all it was meant to do. If you are moderately healthy and twenty – I promise – you are sexy. Do the forty-year-old version of yourself a big favor, and just stinking enjoy your twenty-year-old self, so you don't have to look back and say, "Dang- I was sexy?!?" Just own it for now. Roll out of bed into cutoffs and a tee-shirt with bed head and sleep in your eyes and head to the convenience store for a breakfast of potato chips and an Icee aware that you are a total train wreck, and still the best-looking thing in a square mile. Because – you're twenty. I will now go drink a spinach alge pressed juice... that's how my metabolism rolls these days.

I think I may be becoming my mini-van for a few reasons. One example? I hate high heel shoes. In my twenties they were fine, they were sexy – outfits look far better – wear the heels. Now I walk into work, sit at the desk, take off the heels. Walk into the party, sit at the table, take off the heels. If you see me at a function in town, chances are I'm chatting to you with my feet under the table bare!!!! Shhhhh!!!

I also hate fitted clothes... they make you stand funny, and breath funny, and you have to use good posture. And big earrings kill me! They're so uncomfortable! And a ton of makeup just feels like a mask. I am telling you – I was thinking today about putting on the baggy dress and wearing some sensible shoes. I'm becoming my minivan.

We both are getting a bit worn out; road wear… weather damage. Especially in the front. She's scrapped out her bottom and stuff was dragging around for a week, so we got it together with some twist ties and glue. I've given birth three times… I can relate. She has a front bumper that continually pops out, and you gotta knock it in. My shoulder knows all about that. Recently my husband was commenting on the minivan's shoddy appearance- so I mentioned getting her spruced up, a nice detail service with a bit of paint, a wax, maybe even some nicer rims on the tires. She'd look pretty! That was funny apparently.

The signs that I am devolving into my mini-van became clear last weekend. I went to Walmart in my pajamas Sunday morning. This is true. Before hauling children off to church, I hauled my tired behind into Walmart to grab cinnamon rolls and orange juice. My husband calls sweatpants a: "Walmart tuxedo" … I upped the ante. Pajama pants. When you see that website, "People of Walmart" … and you wonder – "Really??? Who would dress like that?" Now you know. You know someone.

I look at that mini-van and I'm beginning to wonder if those people who care so much about how their car looks aren't a bit wiser than I am? I think maybe I need a different standard in my life. I may not be twenty-year-old sexy, but I think an effort should be made—before the mumu and crocks take over completely.

HORRIBLE... POINTLESS

I had planned on writing about why the horrible, pointless 'Daylight Saving Time' is horrible and pointless (in an amusing yet thought-provoking way), but, I can't. To be remotely amusing, or thought-provoking, I would have to feel a bit amusing or be capable of thinking, and I am not – and cannot. I am exhausted from horrible, pointless, daylight saving time!

Did you know it has nothing to do with farmers? I always heard we needed to move clocks around to help out the farmers. And of course, that makes you feel guilty. Everyone loves farmers – you've got to help those folks. Though you think, 'can't they just set the alarm a bit early and leave the rest of us alone?' But, as it turns out, it was never for the farmers! It was for the politicians! To pay for World War I. Where are the hippies when you need them? Not fighting the patriarchy of war now?!? I'd get behind you guys on this one!

Want a cool list of statistics explaining why daylight saving is destructive, defective, and genuinely deadly? Here you go:

In the days following Daylight Saving Time CNN reported that the risk of stroke was increased by 8 percent! Cancer victims and those over 60 having a 25 percent and 20 percent increase for stroke respectively. Car accidents increase 8 percent according to a Canadian study in 1996, and study by Michigan Medical found heart attacks increase as much as 24 percent! That's a lot of people paying a substantial price for... whatever it is we are supposedly gaining. There are social ramifications as well. Science Daily reported that judges often hand out sentences up to 5 percent longer in the days following Daylight Saving.

While I appreciate giving data to defend my clearly biased- yet undoubtedly accurate statement that daylight saving is utterly pointless and horrible, I need to state the real problem. This column is called 'Thinking Outside the Box' for a reason. I want to think about things from a different perspective. So often in life, we just accept things as they are; because it's just the way it's always been. I wanted to see if we could take a fresh look at something, after all, we might find that what we are doing isn't actually logical. In fact – we might be doing something that's pointless...and horrible.

For example: Taking an hour from March (follow me here) and giving it to October. It's socialized time. Redistribution of hours. March, don't be so greedy. October would really like that hour. Yes, it does belong to you, and it's not really fair, but we are going to forcibly take it—and give it to October. Now, all better?

WE DID NOT DO ANYTHING! The earth is still rotating at the same speed! The actual hours of daylight and darkness did not change! What we did accomplish, by using the contrived device of government policy, is having coerced people into waking up an hour earlier than they wanted to. We did not do this by changing the actual hours of daylight. We simply told them that: Henceforth 7 am will be 8 am. And, if they wanted to wake up at the same ACTUAL time that they had been waking up the day before... then all of the businesses and schools would have to come together and change their hours of operation. No, we aren't willing to deal with that epic debacle! (Although there's usually that random citizen who puts up a fight over every little thing. Usually for no good reason. They just get some adrenaline rush from being annoying. Where are they? Why are they just accepting this clock changing fad?)

So, we risk increased car accidents, sleep deprivation, divorce, stroke, and the death of loved ones all in the name of appeasing our gracious government overlords while pretending we don't know that nothing actually changed!

Now, this is important. It has come to my attention that this column sometimes receives critiques. Apparently, a focus on the amusing is assumed to demonstrate a lack of attention to straight facts and data. I was shocked. I mean, Wow! I know I rarely (never) cite my sources... and I refuse to research beyond the first page of Google. But – this accusation is unfair! This column is solely focused on big issues and is determinedly accurate! It's what you might call, "hardcore journalism." It's legit stuff!!!

And with this in mind – I am going to divulge the truth behind the invention of daylight saving time. This is true: It's the Illuminati. They are establishing a one world order, and using our foggy minds at this time of year to control us!!! I'm serious! Have you noticed that Trump isn't Tweeting?? Don't you think that's suspicious? I know everyone is worried about Russians and Wikileaks, but it's all a smoke-screen! There are reptilian aliens who make big moves with the support of the Free Masons every March. (There's something going about with the sasquatch too. They are major players.) And you just let them! Because for a good week you're just to dang tired to pay that much attention! Shocking? – I know.

I mean, if it's not? Why? Why on earth would we pretend that "Cutting the bottom off of a blanket and sewing it onto the top made you a bigger blanket?" That would be absolutely ridiculous!

(The author is not citing the blanket quote's source... she's not sure where it came from. She stole it from a Facebook meme. She did tell you she is lazy about locating source materials.)

MOST RECENT COMMON ANCESTOR

A few years ago I spent way too much time on Ancestry.com. Have you ever done that? It's a rabbit hole you get sucked into and lose hours of your life looking at photographs of tombstones in imaginary places like, "Vermont." It's a lot of fun and you quickly learn interesting things you didn't know about yourself. For example, your poor relatives are really hard to trace and your rich relatives are easier. And you find the sad truth, that what you really wanted to know is never going to be available. Why does my daughter love tomatoes? Who gave my son his wacky humor? Did any of my relatives give me that sweet feeling I get in my heart when it's raining outside? You want to know that stuff. What you get are names. Weird names. Like Hezzoriah and Batholomias. They must not have had teasing in the 1700's... I think they were too busy - everyone was pretty hungry.

I spent a ton of time growing the ever-expanding branches of my family tree and at one point I got excited! I started seeing words like Duke... Dutchess... and then Princess and then King!!!! "Wow! I can tell my family that we are descendants of royalty," I thought. "No way!" And the King was named John... King John... brother of King Richard. King John who was tormented by some guy named Robin Hood. Because he was such a terrible leader. One of the most famous bad guys in all of history. That guy. I'm one of his.

That was a bummer. But it turns out that 99% of people with even a drop English Heritage are actually decedents of this family. (That's a real fact established by the mathematical equation from a guy named Mark Humphry's – not like Vermont.)

In 1312 King Edward II (King John's grandson) was nearly murdered by frustrated Nobel men. (Kings and nobility were quite fond of killing each other back then... it was like how we really like Instagram). He survived and within a year gave birth to a son, King Edward III. Edward III would go on to have nine children. If you have even the slightest hint of British blood, you are his descendant. And he is not the only person whom a large chunk of the planet is likely related to. It is also argued by some that 16 million men are direct descendants of Genghis Kahn. That's just following strict male to male inheritance. The numbers of those who are genetically related is unfathomable. There are even family trees potentially linking the current British Monarch, Queen Elizabeth II, as a descendant of the Muslim prophet Mohamed.

In fact, the math adds up far faster than you'd assume. According to the infallible expertise of Wikipedia, every single human on the planet likely shares a common ancestor within 3000 years (1000 B.C). How amazing is that? This is largely due to early European voyagers... Magellan, Amerigo, Columbus, Ponce De Leon, etc. These fellas and their fellow seafaring men (there's a joke to be made here... winky face) left their European DNA across the globe. Three thousand-ish years ago, we have at least one individual that every single person on the planet is related to. This person probably wasn't wealthy or fancy. But this is the one person who would wind up on every single person's family tree. In fact, if it weren't for really obscure tribes in the Amazon and such, we could likely find a common ancestor far more quickly. More than likely if you aren't from a rare remote tribe, by 3 thousand years ago we would find hundreds of people who most of us share as common ancestors.

If you want to wander even farther down the family tree, you can search out mitochondrial DNA and Y-chromosomal DNA. These are chromosomes that descend exclusively through women or men. They can tell us the original mother and father of all people. And, I haven't even told you about Neandertals, and Denisovans or Native Australians! Lots of cool stuff!

I'm not certain why I get so fascinated with this stuff. It is, as they say, ancient history. But, it absolutely fascinates me. All the short, difficult lives with their little moments of love and happiness. All the people who smelled freshly plowed dirt enjoyed the warmth of a fire, told a goofy story, struggled over a pot hoping to make a yummy meal. I so want to know their stories. I want to know where that little birthmark came from, or the weird cowlick. I can't help this desire to know those people and appreciate their perspectives. To look around this town and think, we all have far more in common than we often recognize. We are a big weird family. (Unless of course you don't say, "Thank you" when someone holds open a door for you at the store.) I'm NOT claiming those folks as kin.

6 REASONS TO QUIT SCHOOL AFTER 6TH GRADE

I HAVE USED MY DEGREE (A LITTLE). AND I SEE THE value in what I have learned... but I daily help my children with their homework and find myself wallowing in what a complete waste of time it is to think about the stuff they are being forced to study. Not my daughters in elementary school. They are learning multiplication tables and spelling words. You gotta know that stuff. But my teenage son??

I want to march into his school and shout "Hey! We are just killing time until he goes to college, aren't we? Everything he is learning today is useless, pointless, drivel that we will memorize long enough to take your standardized test - prove you taught him something and immediately forget."

Let's just admit it. I hate to harsh your mellow public high school system... but a lot of this stuff is pointless. From the Fibonacci sequence to the countries of the world and their capitals, or the year Colorado gained statehood – we are just killing time.

Most everything I learned after 6th grade I have never ever used. I spent every day from 6th grade until college memorizing stuff long enough to pass a test and then forget it, for literally the rest of my life, with zero consequences. And if you doubt my experience... try to think of a time you used these subjects unless your career is specific to them...

#1 Biology - I am sure I learned something about the mitochondria of a cell being pretty important?? But the only thing I do remember from the class was collecting bugs and stabbing them to a foam board. I am confident I developed arachnophobia in Biology... can't think of anything else I learned... just to fear spiders.

#2 Geometry - Finding the radius of a circle, knowing how to find the volume of a cylinder... I have never ever ever ever done this in real life. I have never once used pi in my real life. If I forgot pi tomorrow and could not for the life of me remember - the impact on my existence? 0. Geometry has done nothing for me ever.

#3 Social studies - I don't even know what we learned in social studies in high-school. I can't even figure out what I would write here in reference to the subject because I have forgotten so much of what I crammed into my brain in order to pass exams (and I was a History major...) Everything I can think of comes from my college education. I suppose the battle of Bunker Hill? That might have been from high school?

#4 English - Does it matter which part of a sentence is the subject vs. the predicate? What about the past perfect participle?? Does knowing the one from the other further your knowledge ever? If you cannot tell by the sound of a sentence whether or not it works, you are likely not clever enough to figure it out by parsing it into literary, philosophical jargon. It has helped no ESL person ever.

#5 Psych? - I think there was a Psychology class in there somewhere. I think I learned that dog's drool if they hear well-timed bells... that's all I got. Hasn't helped.

#6 Chemistry - The only thing I learned in my Chemistry class was that it was really fun to mutter to my friends, "Life sucks and then you go to Chemistry." I do believe there is something about really weird math and electrons were moving around. Times in my life that I needed to demonstrate how ClH_3O combines with H_2Au_6.... Never. Not once.

So... what do they say about the definition of insanity? Not sure why it is we still do education this way. Google seems to have destroyed the idea that shoving knowledge into your brain is a valuable skill – how about kids take more shop classes or coding or how to manage money and what to do with all the weird papers that you need to keep, but not really and where to put them. That stuff will be life changing!

Side note to my teenage son: This is a funny column - don't start taking it literally. It is in no way a reason to believe you can get crap grades and blow off school and accomplish anything meaningful in life. You are NOT Steve Jobs building Apple from the garage while you hang out with hippies. You need to get good grades and a decent job and be a normal functional person. Maybe someday it will help you to write snarky columns in a paper.

HAPPIEST PLACE ON EARTH

We took a family road trip this past week. It was four days of driving for three days of visiting. The highlight of the week was Disneyland. No one is more surprised that Disneyland was the highlight than I am. I went to college in Southern California. I've spent quite a bit of time in Disneyland. I hate it there. It should be called, "spend-a-small-fortune-to-stand-in-hot-miserable-long-lines-for-hours-to-ride-something-that-makes-you-feel-nauseous" land. I'm not a fan of feeling nauseous. It's in my top three least favorite feelings. Along with pain. And fear... which Disney also gave me a hit of... sooo.... Intentionally exposing myself to these feelings seems insane! Dropping a mortgage payment for the opportunity to feel that way? Why??

So, we went to Disneyland and made the most brilliant Disney discovery ever. A nineteen-year-old cousin assured us that he had spent a lot of time in the park and had very strong opinions about where we should go and what we should do. Within seconds we had given him access to the tickets, the fast pass deals, and our collective mind. We would go wherever he told us to go. And you know what? It was brilliant. A 19-year-old kid with a love of rides and a good sense of direction makes for the best Disneyland trip ever!

I did, however, wind up doing a few things I would never, ever, have done had I retrained rights to my brain. For example I believe I may have told you all of my current fear of high things. (I did not always have such a fear, but 14 years of rock climbing with small children seem to have pounded this fear into my head.) So, a ride formerly known as, "The Tower of Terror" would not have made my list. However, we had surrendered our collective brains to the nineteen-year-old, so I paid no attention when we wandered onto a "Guardians of the Galaxy" themed ride. I certainly didn't bother to worry if it had a previous tower themed nomenclature. After all, it's Disney; the rides are generally pretty tame. I didn't think I needed to be concerned.

Upon strapping into a seat next to my six-year-old daughter a screen in front of me displayed some funny clips from a movie... we jerked around a bit, and then suddenly I was falling! My backpack flew up in front of my face, and I gripped my tiny daughter's hand for dear life. My sister-in-law screamed something about hating rides with drops... I screamed something about hell being equated to my current experience. The ride continued a pattern. It would shoot up at spine crushing speeds and then free fall... repeatedly. My husband's glasses disappeared at some point. Taking leave from his face as his head plummeted to the earth. Then, in the chaos, I felt the tiny hand of my teeny tiny daughter as she wiggled out of my grip. I looked over, my head tucked, screaming, as I plunged and jerked to see her laughing with her hands thrown up over her head. I don't know that kid. I cannot relate to her at all.

The 20-minute ride (Don't tell me it lasts 45 seconds. You weren't there... I lived an entire life in that thing.) was plunging and jerking when suddenly, in front of my face, the wall of the building opened up – to display an entire city line below me. We were high, so very high above the city. Just a mean little gut punch from the folks at Disney of what was about to come. Then the doors slammed shut, and in the pitch black - we fell.

The photos afterward have given us so much entertainment. The kid's faces: honestly laughing and thrilled, the grown-up's: in pain. The adults spent the afternoon downing Dramamine and getting the sweats. The kids had a blast.

Disney made the trip far more fun, and I have to admit, I am feeling a bit guilty for having hated on Disney for so long. I suppose many of you who are big fans have had an experience more akin to our 'follow the teenager' plan. It was the highlight of a long family road trip primarily spent in the hot seats of a mini-van.

I do think that Disneyland is completely wrong on their theme, however. Disney claims to be: "'The happiest place on earth." This is NOT true. I found the happiest place on earth. It was a bathroom off of Interstate 15 North after having downed a Vente Vanilla Iced Latte from Starbucks which was followed by clarifying to my husband more than an hour earlier my need to visit a bathroom, while he managed to persuade me that another hour was doable. I have never been happier to be anywhere than I was to be in that bathroom.

This is because what really makes for the happiest place on earth isn't just how pleasant it is; it is also about how desperate you are to be there. Obviously, we are all fairly desperate to spend more time with our families, catching up and making memories. But, that nasty gas station bathroom off the freeway – when you really need it? That is the happiest on earth.

SPRING INTO ACTION

Let's talk about getting outside and enjoying the beautiful outdoors! If there was ever a community with the ability to get our exercise out in the fresh air, it is Montrose.

I mean – not yet. But, eventually.

It's still way too cold and snowy now. But spring is coming!

Soon you can be that lady on the anti-histamine commercial jogging through the flowers.

Of course, if you're like the girl in the commercial you probably need some allergy medication. Those always make me so tired. It's easier just to stay home with one of those fancy air filters. But that's me – you could go and run through the flowers... Well, not really though. I mean, spring around here is more like mud. You'd be filthy and your tennis shoes would weigh a billion pounds from the thick clay (they won't let you into Golds with dirty tennis shoes.) So – I'd put it off for a while.

This summer is better. In the summer you can exercise outside! Just wait 'till summer!

Well – as long as you don't mind skin cancer. You do know Colorado has notoriously high rates of skin cancer, right? Not a lot of atmosphere between your freckled brow and the scorching sun. But if you wear a hat, and a long-sleeved top and lots of thick sunscreen (dripping into your eyes, covered in UV sunglasses that slide down your nose.) Then you could go out this summer.

Maybe even take a trip through the new water park at river bottom. As long as you don't mind the inherent risks associated with rivers. I mean, they don't even come with lifeguards. Can you even?? But, as long as you have a good life vest... which should protect you if you tip but might not. You never know.

Or you could just hike... in the wild... out with the bears and the mountain lions. You might want to bring your bear spray... or better yet a gun. A nice easy trail run with bear spray and a gun... Just to be prepared.

Sometimes people trip and fall.

They do!

Speaking of fall, what you should do is just wait for it. The sun is lower in the sky, the water is lower in the water park. That's when you should go. Although it rains pretty much every day in the fall. You know – Colorado – if you don't like the weather wait five minutes... right? AmIright?

So, fall is better, you'll likely get caught in a storm, but that's ok. You're tough! Get outdoors this fall! It might be a bit chilly and the mud will come back, and you still need your sunscreen. But hey – you moved to Colorado because you're an outdoorsy person! Get out there! I mean, really, what could go wrong?

BARCELONA BABY

"The one thing that unites all human beings, regardless of age, gender, religion, economic status, or ethnic background, is that, deep down inside, we all believe that we are above-average drivers."
— Dave Barry

You are a terrible driver. I know this because I drive and 98% of you are doing it wrong. This may seem ironic as some of you (it has been made clear through inappropriate gestures) believe that I am a bad driver. You are wrong. There are even people (police officers) who have even declared my driving to be definitively bad based on actual data. Data such as speed limits. But, here's the thing, speed limits are pointless. They are dictated by the lowest common denominator of driving.

We do not choose the speed limit based on what a professional Nascar driver is capable of driving. We pick the speed we believe can be driven by the most incompetent driver relative to that particular road. So speed limits, by their very nature, are being determined by our lousiest drivers. And - I am not one of those. Speed limits ought to be something you could opt out of, or at least an exam in which we give speed limits based on your actual ability and relative common sense.

It would be easy enough to weed out the dimmer bulbs among us, a quick scroll through social media can give a fairly accurate IQ assessment. Although... we all know that super brilliant guy that can't tie his shoes, so we need more than just an intelligence exam. I think we need a driving test. Some orange cones in a parking lot might be effective, although I'd recommend, based on personal experience... Barcelona.

I am going to tell you a true story (mostly) that happened to me. I was with my three children driving in downtown Barcelona. The prevailing attitude of the Barcelonaise is: they are driving and if you get in their way you will die. It means that there are about a million pedestrians who avoid being hit by inches. This is because the prevailing attitude of the pedestrians is: they are walking and if you get in their way your car will get bloody. It is the world's most disturbing game of dare ever. No one is giving so much as a nod to the other cars, humans, Vespas that are all careening at breakneck speeds around the streets the size of postage stamps.

I'm such an American... I totally gave. I would panic and slow down. I had a lot of highly accented phrases that I couldn't exactly interpret thrown my direction every time I slowed to avoid running over a child. The comments seemed to be pointing out my incompetence and a few unkind things about my mother.

On the first day of driving, I arrived unscathed at a hotel that I had chosen specifically because the internet declared that it had a parking lot. I drove to the front door and found the sidewalks were all filled with cars already. Yes... I do mean the sidewalks. (The streets are too narrow, so all the cars park on the sidewalks.) I never did find out if that was legal or just so common that no one bothered to care. Finding no parking available for sidewalks several blocks in numerous directions I called the front desk and asked where the parking lot was located? The said it was underground and I would need to check into the front desk in order to obtain the key. I explained that I had tried to find parking near the hotel to no avail and needed to go to the lot. (I did not actually say 'to no avail,' I don't have any idea how to translate that into Spanish) they told me to park in front of the hotel.

Ok. I'm not sure how to explain this. There was no 'front of the hotel.' What there was - was a staircase... going down. I tried to point out that I was driving a car, and the only front of the hotel was a staircase. They said... "Si."

This conversation repeated a few times, interspersed with me whisper-yelling at my son to save me with google translate. I tried in broken Spanish to make it clear that cars are not meant to be parked on staircases. The guy on the phone made it clear that: 'Si. Se puede.'

So I did it. I parked a rental car, in a foreign country... in a stairwell.

Not once, the whole time I was there, did I see a car pulled over getting a ticket. Never. I lived there for six weeks and zero cars ticketed. Think about the sheriff's department landmine of speed traps every time you dare to drive down Chipeta. (Don't do it, it's honestly just too sketchy... they are like vultures waiting for the kill.) But, in Spain, not once did I see anyone who showed any concern for traffic laws or traffic safety. The population at large was driving high speeds through crowded pedestrian filled crosswalks with zero visibility and pin turns and the overall attitude seemed to be... boredom. (Unless I slowed down at all... then the attitude became somewhat hostile.)

You know what else I never saw? An accident. None. The people of Spain are not more intelligent, or more competent. They do not have a special knack for driving. It is just that they have decided that driving will be a skill in which the rules are not set by the lowest common denominator. If you can't pull it off become a pedestrian.

A LOVE LETTER TO MONTROSE

I recently saw a Facebook post from a "friend" (you know what I mean) who said how much he can't stand the "crappy half" of Colorado. He meant us: me and a lot of you.

It may shock you that he regularly spouts off about the backward, intolerant people in the "crappy half" of Colorado. Well. He is wrong. We are NOT the crappy half – we are the AWESOME half. And I'll tell you why.

First Point: We are NOT backward. Do you know how many minorities have been mayor in this town?? Or how many mayors were women?? Or women-minorities? We've got a pretty killer record on that front for such a backwater crew!

And... talk about minorities!! Do you know who owns everyone's favorite shop the Coffee Trader?? Do you know?? That's right – I'll say it...

Asians.

(Disclaimer – I had Phong and Dee check that joke. They thought it was funny – you can laugh.) (Added

Disclaimer, if you aren't a local that joke will not make sense.)

So, I know he thinks that I should be ashamed of my backwater, non-diverse community in which a good third of my kid's classmates are Hispanic, and the wealthy kids are being quizzed on multiplication by their best friends who are getting subsidized lunch. You know, a non-diverse community where ranchers are Democrats, and hippies are Libertarians.

Point number two: We all know why he doesn't like the "crappy half" of Colorado and it's not for our Hispanics, or our special coffee shop owners, no – he judges us for our 'God and Gun's' view of the world, and yes – I will admit, we do vote a little more Texas and a lot less California.

To which I say: "Merica!"

I LOVE Americana. Not like NPR with an, "Aw, let's harken back to the sweet olden tymes of America and quaintness of it all but then stab it up later with insults." Or, just for example—and not at all because I was there and will never ever forgive her—Emmy Lou Harris singing olde tyme hymns up in Telluride and then reminding everyone that while she does sing the olde tyme hymns... she doesn't like 'believe' that non-sense (snort snort). And, not in the hipster-chic ironic Americana - college kids with un-calloused hands wearing a pearl button cowboy shirt as a statement piece. No. Like really. I love good, old-fashioned, American culture.

Yes – every culture has its problems. I mean, driving by the Ute Indian museum makes me feel guilty. Every. Single. Time. Sure Chipeta – we'll name roads and towns after you... but your kids can't – you know – live here.

But, every culture has their good and their bad. We can

enjoy Bollywood and still recognize the problems with the Cast system.

So, I experimented a bit in my twenties, looked it over... played the field. Tried out lots of religions – (a couple looked great on me by the way.) I studied and thought and studied, and for my money- the good old "Love your enemies, bless those who hate you," religion of yon was a compelling fit.

And I'm not ashamed to say that I dig the Constitution and the Declaration. Read them! They're ingenious!

I can quote John Locke's second Treatise, a few of Ben Franklin's snarky one-liners, Jefferson, Washington, and, like any good patriot, I can't stand Hamilton. I've read the Federalist Papers, and I've even read Marx, Nietzsche and other embarrassments to humanity. The logic in Locke's philosophy is solid; it's powerful. If you disagree with me – you're wrong.

Glad to help.

So, that "friend" may think that he shames us with his superior worldview that he learned from Hipster-values.com. But, I think it'd be A-ok for me to just hang with all you uneducated "crappy half" people who just crawled out from under a rock. I like your rock.

THE QUEST FOR THE ELUSIVE SCHOOL SUPPLY LIST

So, I won't be a homeschool mom. The crazy grows strong within me, and I do not want to imagine where the consequences would lead. But, I do envy them. I envy them most when this season begins. Back to school shopping... a journey of epic proportions.

Each school year begins with this dreaded time. An incessant slog for shoes that they will outgrow before the first week is out... and $200 supply lists that each classroom now requires. (Insert grump face emoticon here.)

Remember when you just bought a Lisa Frank Trapper keeper and a backpack? No anymore. Now it is up to us to provide the hand sanitizer and tissues and all the evil folders.

O.M.Goodness!!! The folders!!

With the holes but without the pocket, in paper, not plastic, but with the plastic page covers for the older kid— not the girl. The aisle of the back left corner of Target will be abuzz with the heated, bitter, angst of Moms and Dads yelling, "No! Corbin and Serenity! I told you I needed the yellow folder with the flaps but not the three holes and no plastic! Do you see what this is? It's plastic!"

"But dad it's yellow!"

"I know it's yellow and has the right flaps, but it's plastic. Just go back into the bins the right one must exist, or we wouldn't have been asked for the stupid thing!!"

Dad glances at watch realizing that he has spent half of the day here and still cannot find five things on one kid's list and three items on the other and has not even started on the shoe shopping.

And then the murmur begins to take shape. All of Walmart and Target are abuzz... no one knows... did you ever even see it? It is elusive and terrifying. It binds us all in the common cause. It must exist... but where and why??... The desolation of irritation... the 'art gummy eraser.'

IT DOESN'T EXIST. It doesn't. I have had kids in this district their entire lives and not one year ever did I manage to locate the elusive art gummy eraser. I always hear the timid rumor - that I must leave the hallowed halls of Target and Walmart if I am to locate its presence... whispers abound... you will find that which you seek if you will look to the Depot of Office. But, as I begin the quest, three insane children in tow, raging battles are afoot.

The battle lines are drawn. Who will lay claim to the larger chunk of the family finances? A cute romper for the girl or better shoes for the boy? The littlest is easily played the fool; the older children bribe her with quarters if she abandons her quest for a Dora backpack.

. . .

The air is thick with intrigue... how best to play mom... tell her she's pretty?? (Don't oversell it.) Guilt her about recent trauma's she failed to solve? Whine incessantly? What is the most effective weapon and who will be the first to deploy?

Alas upon arrival at the Depot of Office... alleged home of said elusive eraser the managers of the great land declare that the eraser is 'sold out' and won't be restocked in many moons. The journey is a failure and I hang my head... perhaps (not for sure, but...possibly) I may scream about the stupid romper and if one more person tries to tell me I am pretty I will take away the iPad for a month I-swear-it!

Our band of weary warriors descends upon the oasis of desperate parents, Cold Stone, to assuage my wrath with chocolate and the assurance that the gummy worms are healthy. There has to be fruit in there somewhere.

A truce is reached. No child is getting anything! Mommy is taking the money for therapy.

SMELL YA LATER...

THIS IS DISGUSTING! I MEAN, I'M SURE YOU'VE NEVER done it (I certainly haven't.) On the list of icky or weird- it's just really really really high; the stuff of stalkers and the unsocialized. But, according to the University of Weizmann, you are totally doing this. (Not me, I'm still special.)

What is it? After you shake hands with people... supposedly... (Brace yourselves!) you sniff them! (NOT ME!!) I know... ewww!!

With hidden cameras, researchers at Weizmann interviewed people and videoed them shaking hands. The "sniffing" was always discrete and completely subconscious. People would scratch their faces or rub their chins, but by monitoring air flow and how often faces were scratched when not following handshakes, it soon became obvious. People shake hands and then sniff the chemical traces left by the handshake.

This is especially interesting since we now know that humans are actually capable of picking up numerous subtle clues through our olfactory senses. The tear ducts of women, for example, contain chemicals that inhibit aggression and lower blood pressure when others are exposed. So, if you shake hands with a woman and she has rubbed her eyes earlier she is chemically lowering your blood pressure and calming your mood... just through a quick handshake, and sniff. Fear is also detectable through our sense of smell.

Recent studies also demonstrated that women could smell their best genetic match in a partner, simply by smelling men's sweaty tee-shirts. Without fail, women were able to pinpoint the shirt that had the least similar immune system - giving her future children the greatest genetic diversity. What was more interesting- if a woman was on birth control she no longer could do this. (This makes dating while on birth control a poor choice, should a woman be looking for a life partner.)

Currently, studies tend to focus on the olfactory senses of women. This is due to the findings that women prove more adept at picking up cues through smell. I am a bit doubtful of this current belief. I would hypothesize that it is highly unlikely that men are functioning without pheromone signals affecting them, and far more likely that universities are studying issues that men are not genetically wired for. One of several studies that men failed at was the ability to pick detect their own child's wet diaper from a lineup, just by sniffing them. (Just imagine if men had been good at it. That would do away with paternity tests!)

It seems clear that our bodies are picking up cues from those around us while we aren't often aware. It lends credence to our regular references regarding intuition. Perhaps there is a reason someone "rubs you the wrong way," and you can't quite figure out why. It is possible the instinct you are fighting is grounded in a valid but subconscious knowledge.

Is it possible that we smell deceit? Dishonesty? Do we

perhaps "know" someone is having violent thoughts or intentions after sniffing a handshake, but the reasoning is buried deep in the neurons that we aren't fully cognizant of?

The researchers who studied our handshaking/ hand sniffing tendencies said once you were aware of it, they realized that people were sniffing at things constantly. They said the same behaviors we see in rats with their twitchy noses and hands constantly rubbing at their faces, are seen in humans as well, we just mentally block out those behaviors as visual white noise and so they go unrecognized.

In fact, while we often dismiss our ability to smell, thinking of it as the domain of bloodhounds and other animals with giant olfactory lobes, our noses are proving surprisingly adept when exercised. Researchers found that if students got on their hands and knees and pressed their faces to the ground, they could follow the scent of chocolate around campus much like a dog. This is fascinating, but I have to admit when I heard it... I just... well, I wanted to see it.

Imagine if you will: a university campus (let's just say -it has a legendary reputation.) And at that campus, you would find students on hands and knees with their faces pressed to the ground sniffing. Does that bring up a rather amusing image? And by the way – they practiced their sniffing, quickly improving, to the point that they are on par with dogs at trailing scents. Do you have a campus that you'd be amused to see these awkwardly posed students? Rear ends up in the air as they crawl with their faces pressed to the ground? Anywhere at all that the unusual posture might be a bit extra amusing? (I saw the photos... it's great... science) Well, I won't indulge your shallow, petty desires. It would be immature to mock any school, for what was actually a very informative and interesting study simply because they looked ridiculous doing it. (It rhymes with Shmerkly... shmerkly shmalifornia... the pictures are brilliant.)

Yes. We are sniffers. It is weird and shameful, and icky... our sniffing tendencies. But, whether handshaking or ground tracking our sense of smell is a fascinating line of inquiry. What are we picking up every day that we have been dismissing? What instincts are we fighting that may be far more beneficial than we recognize? It may be too early to know, but in the future, we may find that our creepy animal instincts are far more valuable than we ever realized. And hopefully, we can use our noses standing upright - most of the time.

GOOD FRIDAY

It's good Friday today. It's called Good Friday, but that's a pretty funky twist on the word good. It's a day to focus on death. It's a day to ruminate on the material, the biological. To stare death in the face and honestly ponder the lack of meaning. Today is the day we look down on the earth and face the big fears. How vulnerable we are, how dark life can be. That we are, each of us, a few heartbeats away from rot.

Our town recently made national news with a funeral home and some questionable practices. Most people actually seemed most uncomfortable with the perfectly acceptable sale of body parts. I was listening to a national podcast, "Louder with Crowder," and they were joking about the issue. Again, not anything illegal – but discussing that a body becomes easily butchered and sold and most of us never consider this – because it's uncomfortable. The sale of pieces of people for research was, and is, completely ethical – the grotesque nature is not because it's unethical – it's because we are a people sanitized from the reality of death.

On good Friday we refuse to look away. We acknowledge the death. We remember the evil, cruel, heartless and disgusting. This is the day that we focus on the dark... we give it a good, long, look.

We go ahead and admit that roughly half the country hates the other half of the country. We say we want to get along – we say we want to be tolerant and accepting, but we cannot seem to disagree with each other without hating one another. I can't decide if it's that the media just loves giving voice to the jerks (which I'm pretty sure is true) or if we like to pay attention to them – so the media is just giving us what we want? And I'm no better, lest I paint myself as some middle of the road saint. I am a self-important jerk. I absolutely believe that I am right and those who disagree with me are wrong. This is probably not unique to me, but it's certainly true. I believe in absolute truth... so I believe that one opinion is superior, and one worldview is more effective. If that weren't the case, there would not be successful societies and unsuccessful... successful people and unsuccessful.

On good Friday we admit the weaknesses underlying our hope. In theology there is a philosophical concept known as "the atheist maker." Dostoevsky wrote about it often. It's a logical circle. God is all loving. God is all-powerful. Evil exists. All three of those statements should not be true. Every religion tries to find weird ways to hold all three together. It's like pushing magnets on opposite polls together. Some assert God is not all powerful, some claim God is not all loving. The most shameful solution is always to claim that evil doesn't exist. This is the day that we put that solution to rest. Today we look at the abused and maligned... the hopeless and helpless. We see their pain and acknowledge the injustice of it all.

So what do we do? Do we join the ever-expanding ranks of atheists? Don't doubt me, I see the appeal. I really do. The dark is so deep... the pain is so real. But, that's a good Friday world. It's an Ecclesiastes kind of life. Accept the dark and jump headlong into hedonism.

But, that's cheap. It's the fast-food of worldviews... quick, easy and low in quality. The world is not so simple. The dark and material is not the whole story.

Hope, charity, grace, kindness, love, passion, zeal, prudence, patience... all the glorious and valuable attributes - they exist. There is a purpose...there is meaning. It's not straightforward, it's not easy, and it's probably not universal for everyone, everywhere.

There is joy. It may not be easily won, but in the most difficult moments of life (ironically enough) joy often strikes. There is peace. It's not for the lazy. In a smartphone obsessed, anti-depressant addicted, YouTube fanatical world, it is more difficult; but peace happens. It happens all the time.

There is truth and beauty. Yes, you are a walking sack of meat, just a few heartbeats away from rotting nothing; but this does not faze truth and beauty. And, there's that spark – isn't there?

That something else- that isn't material at all; the dreamer with goals and hopes. The spark of light with purpose and direction. The man who is going to defend abused children, the woman who's going to fight injustice, the child who will sacrifice for others. That isn't dirt – that isn't meaningless. That is life – real, eternal – unimaginably beautiful life.

It's so beautiful it will hurt if you look too closely. That story – that beauty – that's Easter.

But that's for a different day. Today is ashes to ashes -

dust to dust. Today we make penance. Today we look down at the earth and mourn the insignificance. Soon we look up. It's dark now – but take heart – Sunday is coming.

LESSONS IN ROUGH WATER

I am terrified, of pretty much everything—all the time. I wasn't always this way, but I had children, and now I am that terrified chicken little who's positive that the sky is constantly falling. This is a serious problem and it has become even worse being married to an outdoorsy guy.

I have been rock climbing with my children for almost sixteen years and I just cannot tell you the terror I have come to live with. Now, thanks to the water park and some cool new gear from the Surf and Kayak Shop on West Main our family is getting into rafting, kayaking, paddle boarding...

Do you know how much I have to worry about? There are currents in rivers that suck you under, there are things called strainers that will chew up your boat (and the people in it). There are all these big waves known as "rapids" in which you can get flipped and tossed and then sucked into those dangerous currents and strainers and whatnot. Then there are the stories of people waking up in the middle of the night to use the bathroom. A little stumble on a river bank at 3 am... and they are never seen again.

"But, hey! It's all fun! It probably won't happen... it's unlikely. Although it might, it could, you never know. Let's go have some fun!!!" (Insert a terrified emoticon here. And maybe the vomit one.)

Meanwhile, these are my kids. They aren't my wallet or my phone... and if put that on your boat and rafted down a river I'd be a bit nervous. How am I supposed to have fun when it's my kids? I mean, I really really like them!

Alas... I'm trying to learn to tolerate risk - especially with the rafting thing. My family loves it – and honestly, I do too. (Don't tell my husband.) It's a whole lot of fun. Especially if I could do it myself, without needing to have my kids involved in the risks. I am trying to remember that even though my maternal instinct is going nuts... they are probably in far greater danger on the car ride to the river. And, that life isn't about survival... they are supposed to get banged up and take risks and revel in sunshine and fresh air and challenges.

It's just that it's completely illogical and violates every principle of motherhood to willingly put my children into a risky situation, on purpose. Thank God for Dad's who provide a counterbalance to my fears. They will be better adults for having taken some risks and had some adventures... and I am going to just close my eyes, try to have fun and make some memories. (And yes... they will put on lifejackets if they have to go to the bathroom at 3 a.m. That's just good parenting.)

WELL... MAYBE NOT SUNSCREEN.

Does anyone remember the letter to the class of 1999? You probably heard it on the radio. (It was written in a column for the Chicago Tribune and later put to music.) It would have been viral, but this was before viral. This was when the internet was still mostly for email and you had to listen to it go beeeooohhhhbeeeoooohhhhbeeecc..kckckck-ckckkckc.... deedlllleedlllleedlllldeee......kckckckck and then you could log on.

Here's a small section of the original column by Mary Schmich: **Class of 1999 Wear Sunscreen**

Ladies and Gentlemen of the class of '99. If I could offer you only one tip for the future, **sunscreen** would be it. The long-term benefits of sunscreen have have been proved by scientists whereas the rest of my advice has no basis more reliable than my own meandering experience...

Enjoy the power and beauty of your youth; nevermind; you will not understand the power and beauty of your youth until they have faded. But trust me, in 20 years you'll look back at photos of yourself and recall in a way you can't grasp now, how many possibilities lay before you and how fabulous you really looked. You're not as fat as you imagine. Don't worry about the future, or worry, but know that worrying is as effective as trying to solve an algebra equation by chewing bubblegum. The real troubles in your life are apt to be things that never crossed your worried mind; the kind that blindsides you at 4pm 4 on some idle Tuesday. Floss. Stretch. Be kind to your knees; you'll miss them when they're gone. Maybe you'll marry, maybe you won't, maybe you'll have children, maybe you won't, maybe you'll divorce at 40, maybe you'll dance the funky chicken on your 75th wedding anniversary...whatever you do, don't congratulate yourself too much or berate yourself either – your choices are half chance, so are everybody else's. Read the directions, even if you don't follow them. Do NOT read beauty magazines; they will only make you feel ugly. Get to know your parents. Be nice to your siblings. Work hard to bridge the gaps in geography and lifestyle the older you get, the more you need the people you knew when you were young. Advice is a form of nostalgia, dispensing it is a way of fishing the past from the disposal, wiping it off, painting over the ugly parts and recycling it for more than it's worth. **But trust me on the sunscreen...**

Isn't that awesome! I think it's one of the greatest columns I've ever read (sorry Mr. Barry.)

Most everything she said in her column still holds to this day. Except for the thing about the sunscreen. See, chemical sunscreens were all that we had in the 90's (except the lifeguards with their white noses.) And these chemical sunscreens are still around. They are the nice ones, the ones you can spray, that smear on clean. (The ones you actually like.) These sunscreens – are starting to get a bad rap- a very bad rap, and for a couple reasons:

#1. Chemical sunscreens (for lack of a better term) contain estrogenic properties. Slathering up your kid in sunscreen will expose them to the equivalent estrogen levels as found in a hormone replacement therapy patch. These sunscreens are still available and recommended by the FDA and Dermatologists though. This is because while they know the estrogens are being absorbed, they believe that most of the hormone is excreted in the urine without damaging effects. However, a 2012 article in the International Journal of Andrology found otherwise, and regardless of whether or not we absorb the estrogens to a harmful level through the skin, these hormones are then washed off the body, flushed down the sewer and added to the drinking water where they are not filterable. A more recent article in Environmental Science and Technology also found a strong likelihood that sunscreen can be linked to increased risks for endometriosis and infertility in women. These may prove in peer review to be harmless... but I'd not want to place odds on it.

#2. The other problem? Vitamin D is more important than we realized in the 90's, and the sun is far and away the best source. Not only will too little vitamin D shrivel your bones, and inhibit your immune system... A recent study from Mayo Clinic of Minnesota found low levels of vitamin D increased mortality from all causes including dementia, heart disease, and several cancers.

On a positive note, mineral-based sunscreens (which, thus far, seem to be perfectly safe) have gotten far more pleasant and effective. (My current favorite is Joshua Tree SPF 15).

At the end of the day, we are all doing our best to make wise choices with our health, which as Ms. Schmich pointed out to the class of '99 – are half chance. A few decades ago margarine was healthy. Now it's the devil. DDT was good for us until it was killing us. Traditional sunscreen, well, it's starting to have some issues. Ironically, Mary Schmich was right in her advice about everything. Except for the sunscreen.

LIES AND MISERY... AND DAIRY PRODUCTS

"There's only one thing I hate more than lying: skim milk. Which is water that's lying about being milk."
Ron Swanson - Parks and Recreation.

An ode to skim milk:

Oh, Skim milk – how you disgust me. You are a grey swirl of weakness that invades upon the joy of the day.

You are not creamy. You do not pour forth with a thick, cool, swirl of happiness to crackle upon my cereal or soften my Oreo.

No. You are thin. Weak.

You taste of cardboard and sadness. While you may be lower in calories, you are lower too in purpose. You cannot be whipped with sugar, and you do not satisfy in coffee. You are a bitter pill for the dieting soul to swallow in the desperate desire to have their cake and eat it too.

But, they cannot eat their cake - because their cake tastes sad with skim milk.

Your flimsy, thin, soulless existence is a reminder to all that the civilized life of iPods and indoor air conditioning has come at a tremendous cost.

A terrible, terrible cost.

We can no longer drink our milk as women should. Straight from the pail, wiping the cream off of the top with a swipe of a rugged finger. No. We are lost in a morass of civilization. We have too easy of lives, too few calories burned, and too many easy calories consumed.

So we stare into the abyss of the tinny film of skim milk. The sad price that success hath wrought.

Take heart; oh skim milk. Though you move me to tears with your lackluster existence, you are not the bleakest of essence.

That would be soy milk. Which isn't milk – it's beans.

I SEE YOU

I see you... every day. In dusty work pants, You had to get off early and you don't want to upset your boss so you tried to work extra hard, got in a bit early and took a short lunch because you had to pick up your kid. I see you when that little boy runs into your arms, round face grinning. I watch you ask him about his day, and nod to his teacher learning he still is getting in trouble for being too loud and wiggly... and you know he got that inability to sit still from you, and you have no idea how you'd fix it, but you are proud of him and will keep on trying. You grab his hand and march to the truck and head home. I see you, and I know it's all a struggle, and I see you doing your best. And I admire you. I just want you to know.

I see you jogging up the bike path. You put on way too many pounds this winter. Everything is jiggly as you run. Nothing about you looks like a svelte, twenty-something athlete training for her next half marathon. You look awkward and pained, yet you go. Fighting for your health, your sanity, maybe a pair of shorts you want to fit into. And

I see you jog past. And I admire you... and I want you to know.

I see you... a family of five, holding hands through the parking lot – trying to keep the kids safe -trying to be a good parent. I see you... divorced, hurt, a bit ashamed... but sitting together at the game, just for a bit, so your daughter has her cheering section together for a moment. It's painful, but you love her more than you resent one another. It's so hard and so brave. And I see you.

I see you holding the door open for that person coming up behind you, just to be nice. I see you look up from your shopping cart and smile when we make eye contact—just to be friendly. I see you let that car pull out in front of you. I see you bringing the snacks to class, volunteering to coach, teaching Sunday school, picking up garbage along the street. Every single day—I see you.

On a cold, snowy morning, when I didn't even want to get out of bed, I saw you holding the crosswalk sign to help children cross busy sections of town. Standing out in the cold day after day after day. The kids are safe- because of you. Because you showed up and did a good job. I see you. I want you to know. And I'm very grateful.

In this town, every day, most everyone is doing good. Working hard. Going without trips, or a nicer car or a better outfit to provide for children. Heading to work in the dark and cold, picking up kids late at night from band practice, changing the oil for a neighbor, helping a teacher with a struggling student, visiting a retirement center to volunteer. All over this town, most everyone is working. Trying, in our own small way, to make it a bit friendlier, and bit prettier, and bit more fun.

We all see the ones who don't. Who spend their days complaining. The ones who scowl if you make eye contact, who head to social media to lament their latest gripe. You have to see them. They work very hard to be seen. Longing to spread a bit of pain and destruction everywhere they go. But not you. Not you, and not the vast, vast majority of this population.

There are no trumpets, no big awards, no fancy titles. No one will go on social media to declare the awesomeness of the that people showed up to work and did their best. No one will announce the names of every volunteer coach, and remind us of the late nights, the dinners missed, the unfinished homework, to coach children. No one throws a party when a door is held open, or a thank-you is uttered. There is no reward for choosing to smile at strangers. These actions are profound in how they change our community – but they won't ever come with the awe and enthusiasm they are worthy of.

But, I wanted you to know; all this week, I paid attention. I made a list: 'Kindness.' The list was too long; it was too hard to keep. It was a constant, incessant, barrage of good people making this town a better place.

They say gardens are a testament to the care they get; planting, watering, pulling weeds. It's easy to destroy. Anyone can ruin one. Just leave it alone. A nice garden takes effort, time, consistency; and this town is a lovely garden... you just have to step back from your work now and then to appreciate it. Every day, just a bit better than the day before. Because every single one of you was doing your part. And I see you.

FAMILY AND FITNESS

Everyone has their own way of staying active. Lots of locals use mother nature. With winter approaching, snow-shoeing, cross country skiing, ice climbing and many other outdoorsy activities will become common their sources of fitness.

I have my own activities. I made some little people (three of them) and they keep me on the move. And it's not toddler's I'm chasing. No, they are old enough that they don't need to be pushed in a swing or protected under the monkey bars... (or I'm lazy enough that I just stopped doing those things). No, it's not the active life of a mom with toddler's I'm talking about – it's the older kid activities that keep me in shape now.

Specifically, hiking the stands.

You know what I mean fellow parents. First a mile walk from the parking, then it's up the stadium, then down the stadium – go across the football field to go to the bathroom – the other direction to get to concessions. Up again to find the daughter we let run off with friends, back down again to visit a co-worker.

I am a professional parent/fan/cheer-section, working out aficionado.

You doubt me, but I really do use the stands to my advantage. For example, my rear end goes completely numb while I'm watching (let say gymnastics this time) and my only recourse is to not sit any longer. So, get out of the seat and start walking the bleachers... upstairs and over to the un-even bars, down to the balance beam section and back. Perhaps I'll grab a friend's fussy baby and bounce her a bit to help out since I'm walking anyway.

That's another reason you have to keep moving. I have two other children who are also sore in the rear... and bored. So, a new game is created. "How fast can you go up and down the bleachers 3 times? I'll time you!"

(I totally don't time them – I just make up a number. Shhhhhh.)

"You did it in 73 seconds!!"

And when they are getting antsy, I jump in and race them a few times.

"Oh, look you beat me again! Darn! Now sit down and watch your brother!"

It's also important to make laps around the bleachers because you are freezing!!!

Speaking of which... Oh my holy moly! Marching Band competition in Colorado Springs was epic! Both for the fact that Montrose took 6th!!! (Woohoooo!!! Go Montrose!!) And because we almost died in the ridiculous negative 1000-degree temperature waiting for some school from 'almost Kansas' to win an award and take ten minutes worth of pictures.

(I'm kidding obviously – it was only negative 50-ish) But honestly... those guys need to get a little hustle in their hineys when it comes to band awards – (go visit a KJ

Almgren gymnastics competition here in town.) Just sayin' —things get done.

But, if I could beg of you all, if you have a kid in sports there's no reason not to join me and just do laps on those bleachers... they certainly are not a pleasant place to sit for any length of time, and it will make my kids less uncomfortable when their mom is running up and down the bleachers... singing 'Eye of the Tiger,' ...doing my signature pistol fingers to all the other spectators. Here's the thing: You know I'm cool – and obviously I do- but my kids seem to have some doubts... so a few more stadium hikers will demonstrate the cool factor to my children. As much as they think my bleacher workouts are embarrassing – they have yet to try to talk me into staying home and skipping their performance. No matter how uncool, kids always want us to watch.

SHAME

"Shame. Boatloads of shame... Day after day... Always the same..."

That song by the Avett Brother's was running through my head with every single step. Every single step of the hike up Mt. Huron with a big group of friends. I was ashamed because I was the weak link... I was falling farther and farther behind. Not just falling behind a bunch of adults who are definitely cooler and more Patagonia-outdoorsy than me. - Nope. I was ashamed because I was falling further and further behind the children, lots of children. Nine children. Young children. My seven-year-old daughter summited a good hour ahead of me. No joke. I couldn't even see her most of the hike.

It's so hard to be terrible. It's hard to have a positive attitude and a good sense of humor when you are an utter failure. And you both don't want to inconvenience those around you, and you want to be honest and apologetically aware that they are all a bit miserable because everyone is stuck waiting on you, but you also don't want to make everyone uncomfortable by constantly apologizing and belaboring the issue.

Then I doubled down on my annoying-ness. (It's a word.) I tweaked my foot on the way down. Not sure exactly how – or what was wrong, but it hurt unless I walked on the outer edge of my foot. So, the summit, which was a humiliating sufferfest, – was followed by the descent. A slow, arduous, drama filled shuffle... And - I just kept hearing the song repeat over and over...

"Shame... boatloads of shame... day after day... always the same."

Don't get me wrong. I have some gifts and abilities. I'm not actually an altogether humble person. In fact, some might claim that I'm a bit of a conceited-know-it-all. I generally roll in the: "far too confident and self-assured and maybe even think a bit too highly of myself" category. Most the time.

I probably needed a good smack in the face with some shame. So – yeah me – Karma's on track! In fact, I think all of us are needing some of the shame lessons. I think even you, dear reader, might need a whack to the side of the head as well.

My kids have taught me this valuable lesson. My kids have had days where they were awesome – they know the good days. The day they won the award – maybe not first, maybe third – but still a sense of accomplishment. They have also had days where they got dead last. They have been crying on the car ride home after a terrible practice, frustrated with their incompetence, bitter at their inability to understand an academic skill that everyone else seems to have mastered. Every one of my kids has been the worst in the room... several times. And every time I am a bit grateful. Because life is not a race to be won – it is a journey with ups and downs. And the truth is: the best aren't the most talented or intelligent or even the hardest working. The secret to much of life is getting back up after failure. It is knowing that tomorrow you will be a bit better than you were today and having the fortitude to keep hammering. (Hat tip Cameron Hanes...)

I'm grateful when my kids fail, because those days are the most important. Those are they days that they learn to handle failure and disappointment without giving up – and nothing they learn in sports, or art, or school will be more important than that! (Except for good manners – those might be more important... they are at least equally so.) I may love supporting my kids on the bad days, letting them cry through their frustrations knowing the lessons they learn are worth all the heartache. But I did NOT like facing my shame when it was my turn to fail. That's painful!

So – today – whatever you are facing or have been facing, if you are finding yourself so far below the bell-curve, just know that all of us are there often. And the odds are extremely high, that if nothing else, you are a superior hiker to me! Hashtag winning! And if it all seems too depressing? The Avett Brothers have a good song to share in your heartache – and it's a catchy tune for hiking.

NEW YEAR'S RESOLUTIONS

New year's resolution time! I'm going to stop procrastinating... as soon as I finish mailing the gifts sitting in the office. After that, I will (for sure) quit this terrible habit of procrastinating. I will also work out. Like that burpee challenge I decided to take. I'm three days into the challenge. Number of burpees I've actually done? Zero. But – hey, I'm going to work out... I just need some time first... I've been too busy... not doing burpees... or mailing Christmas gifts.

I also vow to eat right – soon. The bacon burger from last night didn't count, obviously. Very soon I will drink green smoothies and eat lots of kale and yogurt.

I am also going to quit nagging my kids and start speaking to them in a reasonable, calm manner. I will be a dignified mother who can ask her kids to, say, pick up after themselves and when they don't (because they never do) I will not throw a fit and freak out, I will respond with a cool eye raise and take their favorite device away and then, when start driving me nuts because I have taken away their devices and now they would like me to entertain them, I will not cave and simply give them back their devices! I will remain firm and convince them to entertain themselves.

This year I will be less of the normal me, and more of the cool me I imagine in my head. I will stop yelling every single morning as I get my kids out the door... I will stop nagging and complaining... I will start getting on top of my stuff instead of waiting until the last minute.

Or maybe... maybe I will admit that I sometimes I eat too much because I'm celebrating with my family and that's a good thing. Maybe I will admit that while it is obnoxious that my house is a mess, it will soon be empty, and I will miss these days terribly... just like I miss those sleepless nights with a baby on my chest. Maybe, even though I will try not to procrastinate, and try to eat well and exercise – I will also admit that I will not live forever and a good book, chocolate and cheese are not worth missing out on just to have a smaller rear end.

If I'm honest there is a lot that I would probably be wise to get a handle on, and I will work on them, but I know that what actually matters most is getting in more cuddle time on the couch with my husband, spending more hours cheering on my kids and sitting together at big carb laden dinners. Because, this life is passing far too quickly, and my biggest goal is making memories with the people I share a home with – and to be honest, when it comes to loving them, I'm killing it! How about this: New Year's resolution 2018 – keep enjoying the baajeezes out of this family. (And really, get those packages mailed.)

FINDING YOUR BLISS

This week Valley Health is focused on "finding your bliss." This seems to me - to be a subject I am ill prepared to write on. I could write (for example) on finding your "status quo." Maybe finding your "pretty good" or "the kids are healthy and the house is almost clean." I think those are lessons I am well versed in and have some advice to parlay. But finding "your bliss" seems a bit out of my wheelhouse.

If I'm honest I think if it's in your wheelhouse then you sound a bit pretentious. I cannot yet envision the conversation in which someone explains to me that they have discovered "their bliss" in which I'm not feeling a bit judgmental of that person. It feels like a statement that is esoteric enough as to feel like only a truly obnoxious person would have "found it."

Maybe I'm reading too much into it? What if we decided that finding your bliss really WAS finding your status quo? What if it's as simple as having good friends and family? Working hard and being proud of what you've accomplished? Knowing that what you do has purpose and merit?

I think every single job I have had was difficult in its own way. I know I often dreaded going to work – but I also was often proud of what I did... Whether it was waiting tables, changing diapers, patrolling a campus, cleaning a kitchen, calming a passenger, or waking up at three am with a baby... I liked the feeling I had when I'd done my job. I was proud of myself for not giving into my laziest impulse and instead getting into the business of fixing, cleaning, helping. I never came close to curing cancer, or solving the Mid-east crisis, or even getting a local law fixed. But, I have gone to bed, most nights – knowing something in the world was a bit better because I showed up and did what I could to help... and honestly – isn't that what finding our bliss really ought to be? It's a short life. We aren't really here for long. If we pulled our weight... did the part that we could to lighten the load and move things forward, I think we'd know the deep true happiness that life has to offer. Bliss??? That sounds a bit rich – but if we mean a deep, thorough joy from a life with purpose... yeah – I think most of us have found our bliss. And if you are one of the takers?? Consider joining the giver side. There is a deep happiness that you are missing... some might even call it bliss.

WORKING OUT

There has got to be something better to do than work out. Anything.

When I know I need to head to the gym I wrestle with a moment similar to Jim Carry's *The Grinch*:

The gym?

"Even if I wanted to my schedule wouldn't allow it!

1 p.m.- Wallow in self-pity.

4 pm.. – Stare into the abyss.

6 p.m. – Solve world hunger... tell no one!

7 p.m.- Dinner with myself – I can't cancel that again!

8 p.m. – Wrestle with my self-loathing.

I could move self-loathing to 9 o'clock... but what would I wear??"

I know I know IknowIknowIknow!! Fitness is important. It fights depression and arthritis and makes you look good and feel better and sleep better and live longer. Etc. etc.

And we all know a person who has given up. The guy who has abandoned any desire to live or achieve and has molded a permanent groove into a couch where he wiles away the remaining years of his existence allowing the television to drain his motivation as he fades into a bag of Doritos and meaninglessness. (I would now like you to mentally insert the soundtrack from Nirvana "entertain us... here we are now... entertain us...") Thanks.

So, if we grudgingly must acknowledge that, as much as we resent those trainers with their motivation and Paleo diets, we probably do need to get our bodies into shape. But, we can at least acknowledge that we aren't happy about it? So, what's the best way to go about it? Well, if you were to google "What's the best exercise?" The answer that those hard bodies in fitness land would give you is... "The one you'll do."

You know what I would do? I would be the running back for a women's flag football league! I did that in college and it was fun! I would also join a square dancing club in a heartbeat – or a ballroom dancing club... that provided dance partners of course. See. The work out world is obviously conspiring against me - or such options would be available.

To make matters worse, we have to live among those undesirables... you know the people I'm talking about. They find joy in ... – ...running. *shudder*

They run!!! I cannot think of anything more miserable than running. Every single step I am thinking of a million reasons to stop stepping. Here's the mantra in my head. "5... 6...7... I need to stop!... no... 9...10...11.... I need to stop!!...21...23...24... I lost my place... I need to stop! I hate running!... 36...37...38... eleventy-two....??!!!

I cannot think of anything more miserable than running. (Ok, I can. Swimming. Swimming is hell. Swimming is running where you can only breath at special times.)

I have tried running. My husband (with his body fat of

like 2%) keeps assuring me that there is this magic moment where you like it. I have never ever found that moment. Seriously. I believe it is a fictitious lie that good runners use so as to keep crappy runners out there shuffling along so they can snicker at us and feel better about themselves. Jerks.

I did find a workout I enjoyed. CrossFit. I loved CrossFit. If you're looking for a great workout that will challenge you Montrose has CrossFit Agogee, Ouray has CrossFit Hypoxia and Delta has CrossFit... Awesome. (Seriously Delta?? – that name?) But, I am now injured out of CrossFit. It happens.

We have a lot of workout options in this town. Yoga, several gyms, the rec center.

I'm currently at Golds. This is where all the moms are. There is childcare and there are classes with other moms. It's a good fit. I recommend it.

Now, the moment you've been waiting for: my fitness regimen - because (and please read this with a high degree of sarcasm) all of you Montrosians who have seen me wandering through Walmart trying not to road rage over my fellow Christmas shoppers, blocking my access to the butter, and were wondering, "How on earth is that lady so impressively fit?"

I walk... I hate running... but I can walk like nobody's business, and while I'd like Montrose to double its walking access (Townsend – Hillcrest – Chipeta –Rio Grande – Main street??? Shouldn't they be walkable??) Regardless, the bike paths only leave you stranded a handful of times and you can usually hop a few fences and get somewhere. Walking is pleasant. So I walk.

I also have a very intense and important weight lifting regiment. It has one goal: GOAQAP

Get out as quickly as possible.

I walk in, find the heaviest things I can lift. I lift them a few times. I leave.

You are now laughing at my nonsense workout now – but there is a method to my madness. As you chortle over your superior exerciseriness and my ridiculous choices, I shall humble you with my science!

High Intensity Training (google it) has been around for decades and actually is similar to CrossFit in several aspects. It builds muscles quickly and effectively.

It turns out that when doing a heavy lift, at or near your maximum capacity, your body floods your system with human growth hormone. This is the hormone that you are swimming in from 12 to 20. It's the stuff that makes you a lean teen ready to plow through linemen or obsess over video games. It is a hormone that is desperately lacking as we leave our teenage years and it slowly abandons us year by year. Some people even start injecting the stuff to try to maintain their fitness, but a faster, easier way to get some is to do a really heavy deadlift – or even two! (A dead lift is simply taking a very heavy weight and picking it up off of the ground.) That's it. But you can hurt yourself really easily picking up heavy things. So, you should get professional advice when doing it. That said. Pick up a super heavy weight and set it down. Workout over.

It's not too good to believe, this is actually a thing. High intensity workouts build muscle quickly, increase growth hormone dramatically, change your metabolism and – follow me closely hear – they end really quickly. In and out in 20 minutes (or less). Boom. Mic drop.

You're welcome.

DEPENDS WHAT YOU MEAN

Language is funny. I mean you string a few sounds together and give it a meaning. It started with grunts and gestures that we gave some symbolism. From these came sounds like: "Mom" or "Danger" or "If-you-don't-put-down-the-cell-phone-right-now-I-swear-I-will..." All just different noises – strung together in different ways, and yet they can have profound meanings.

It may just be a few letters, but, "We hold these truths to be self-evident..." changed the world. In fact, you would have no cell phone, no computer, no polio vaccine if not for the culture that had evolved around those words. Words like, "Dear Herr Gemlich," brought about world war, while words like, "Tear down this wall!" ended war without a single bullet. We are frivolous with them, because they are common and silly and get us into drama on Facebook, but words do more to change the world than we give them credit for. Ideas are the axis of reality; the illusion otherwise is our own.

This is why we say the pen is more powerful than the sword. A nice cliché, although it has its faults. I can walk through town with a pen and no one will feel threatened (even if I point it at people and yell, "Expelliarmus!") But, if I walk downtown with a sword? I have a feeling I may get a bit more attention.

So, although I am just writing a few silly words, in truth I'm wielding a wild and wonderful weapon. You would think with such power that they would be dependable – these words. It may come as a surprise then, that words often change their meanings. You'd hope something as important as the actual agreed upon definition of a word would be fairly concrete – we don't want these meanings to be so malleable that when I say a word you may believe I mean something completely different than what I intend. Yet it has happened and continues to do so.

For example, the word SOON. (The blessed put off for parents everywhere.) Yes, Billy the child, we will go... soon. Meaning eventually. Soon comes from the Old English word Sona... meaning?

Immediately.

Now - how on earth did SOON come to mean: "very much not immediately so leave me alone!"

Well, I'm guessing... overuse and under follow through? For example: Mothers everywhere said, "Be there immediately," and then showed up a while after immediately. (As is often the case.) And slowly the world came to recognize; when we say, "SOON" ...it's going to take us a bit.

You may think this seems crazy – but it is happening, even today. There is a word... a word you know... a word you likely use – and you have watched it devolve from what it meant – to the exact opposite of what it meant. "No," you think, "I would have noticed such a thing." Ah – but dear reader... you have. Literally.

(That's the word.)

Webster's Dictionary recently had to alter the word's definition to add its current meaning. "Mom! I'm LITERALLY starving!" "I LITERALLY cannot believe that guy did that!" "I LITERALLY need that!"

Nope. You aren't, can, and didn't. You mean figuratively. "Mom! I'm figuratively starving!" "I figuratively cannot believe that guy did that!" "I figuratively need that."

It's literally changing and every day it continues to fade.

Someday in the future, people will be surprised to find that LITERALLY once defined truth, commanded factual support. It will no longer, and we will have been the generation who saw its demise.

So, watch your words... wield your weapon with care. It could literally be life or death... depending on who reads them. Or figuratively. Kind of depends.

LET YOUR LIGHT SHINE

I was oohing and ahhhing over Christmas lights the other night, and my daughter asked me if I was jealous of all the pretty light displays. I am not. I am lazy and so my Christmas lights are veering toward "understated" elegance. (Wink wink). There isn't much in life as selfless as putting up Christmas lights around your home. Christmas lights are a gift you give your neighbors. They're a gift you share with strangers and people you will never meet, who will never thank you. There are homes in this community that I will drive in wakadoo patterns in order to swing by and see their displays. There is a house that's not on Chipeta... but not far off either – and I crane my neck every night trying to get a better look.

That home near Centennial Middle School?? That house wins. At least, that's my son's take on that home – they just win all the holidays. This choice – to light up your home for everyone around you to delight in; it is the most selfless, thoughtful, beautiful gift to your community. You are choosing to fascinate little children, to give every tired adult after a hard day's labor a bit of sparkle and fun.

These are the little things that we choose to do, aren't they? To hold open a door for the person behind us, give a smile to a stranger, laugh at the inconvenience instead of grumble. Every day we can choose to buy in just a bit more. Share the burdens and lighten the load, add kindness and joy to the town we live in. People who put up Christmas lights are the good guys. They have to be. They are choosing to add beauty and sparkle and wonder. No one provides the lights, pays for the electricity. No government agency spends hours hanging, stapling, balancing on ladders. They are giving to our town, donating in a way that will never be written off on their taxes, or recognized with an award. These are the quiet heroes among us that we all are so lucky to be in community with.

This is the time of year when we all need to focus on the "good news." To remember the man who taught us to love our neighbors. Light displays are such a tangible way we love our neighbors. How better to celebrate his birth, his teachings, his world, his good news?

Too often I am the Grinch. I cannot tell you the absolute vitriol that roiled through me when Wal-Mart began selling Christmas stuff in mid-October. I'm not kidding. I was livid. My poor family got to hear a litany of my angst in destroying the Thanksgiving holiday by foisting Christmas on us in mid-October. And that's just the anger I can feel toward my local Walmart. We should talk politics sometime! (Just kidding – that's a bad subject. I'm right and a lot of people are wrong, and it makes everyone uncomfortable to hear how wrong they are.)

But, even a Grinch like me can help out. I did get some paltry Christmas lights thrown up. The easiest, 'plug it in and walk away' version of lights I could manage, but I got some up. I do not hold a candle to many of you however. I could make a list of my favorite homes, and the list would go on for pages. There are homes here in town that make me cry – true story – with their pretty lights. Here's to every single one of you who went out of your way to light up our town and make your neighborhood more bright and fun and festive. Christmas is more special because of you, and we all owe you a debt of gratitude.

"So, let your light shine before men! That they may see your good deeds and glorify your Father in heaven." Jesus of Nazareth - Matthew 5:16

VEGETARIANS

I'm going to tell you a secret. You are a bit jealous of vegetarians. I know – you think that's funny. Because how could you be jealous of a life without bar-b-que? There is nothing on earth as yummy as steak. Or a hamburger – medium, with grilled onions. Or, fried chicken, cold from the fridge at three am... or spaghetti with meatballs! I can go on like this forever! Pork chops with apples! Thanksgiving turkey with gravy. No one can be jealous of missing out on that!

But – I'm telling you that I'm pretty confident that you are still, just a tiny bit, jealous of vegetarians.

'But!' (you tell me) 'I'm not jealous of them! I don't even like vegetarians... they are really high maintenance!' But I'm telling you – I think you're jealous. And – I am too.

Why? Why are we jealous of people who can't eat bacon? BACON??? Sizzling, hot, crackly bacon!?!

Because vegetarians wield self-control like Excalibur. And you and I... we do not.

I'm not sure what it is precisely but we are jealous because they are demonstrably in control.

What's the hang-up for you? Maybe you cannot stop smoking; not for your health, not for your children, not for you family. You literally have nothing in your life that you love enough to just quit smoking – and here this vegetarian has the self-control to give up bacon, not because their life depends on it... just because it's a nicer for pigs. With very little benefit to themselves vegetarians show us just how lacking so many of us truly are.

Perhaps you can't get to sleep without a pack of beer, or you cannot stop over eating, or even undereating; even though you promise yourself that, 'Really, this time, you'll get your health under control.' Or maybe you cannot stop yelling at your spouse, or your kids. Maybe you just can't stop nit picking your co-workers or gossiping about your family or making a jerk of yourself on Facebook. I don't know what it is for you, but there is probably something, and constantly you are struggling to win against your weakness. Then, here comes a vegetarian who doesn't have to give up meat to save their family, or to save their health, or fix their marriage or to just not be a jerk. Nope. Vegetarians simply believe it's kind; and they have that much self-control. So, you feel a bit ashamed – and a lot jealous. Or at least I do.

There is a reason almost every faith requires eliminating something. From pork, to caffeine, alcohol, meat... join a religion and you'll likely need to sacrifice something you love. But, I think that's the genius of organized religions. Sacrifice pays in dividends. It really truly makes you better. And part of the reason – not all, but part – is that sacrifice exercises self-control. Self-control is vital. Period. It's the key to almost everything, and when you join up with a faith, you will be asked to start practicing some self-control.

So, hurray to the vegetarians. Sure, eating more plants

seems to be a good thing. I think we all know we don't get enough of our food from plants in this country. But, hurray for the strength of character that is required to hold yourself to a vegetarian standard. I admire you... we all do. Even if we tease you for being high maintenance... Because... well, there is that.

THE DRINKING AGE IS ALL WRONG.

Many a 19-year-old has wondered why on earth the drinking age is set so high... and we (who are in the legal bracket) roll our eyes. After all, when the federal government raised the legal drinking age... (what?? you claim the drinking age is set by the states? Alas... you are correct, but the Federal government can refuse to send our income tax dollars back to our communities if we don't accept their drinking age limit... and so... the legal drinking age, in America, has been set at 21 years by the federal government.)

Well, once the legal age was set at 21 years vehicle deaths diminished. And, as we know, it's not just the intoxicated driver who dies in these accidents, it is those he or she plows into. In a valiant effort to decrease these senseless fatalities, young people had to surrender their alcohol. And it worked, many of us are alive today because of this very law. But, does that mean it's the best choice?

Every single encroachment upon our freedoms begins with the same altruistic phrase: "If just one life can be saved by...." And lives are saved, and freedoms are sacrificed.

Today, with statistics improving, the drinking age is set to twenty-one.

Now... for an irony, let us just acknowledge that in this country you can responsibly choose to give your life for your country while still not being responsible enough to have a beer. This commonly held belief alone should give us pause.

If a person is not old enough to be capable of making wise choices about alcohol... are they capable of making wise choices about giving over years of their lives in service to their country? Or, perhaps, could we look at it another way: Assuming that a person at eighteen IS capable of making a choice about how they live and the risks they take, why do we accept that alcohol is not a substance they have the logic and self-control necessary to use?

And, could it not be safely assumed that if we made alcohol illegal for everyone age 40-44 that drunk driving accidents would also drop as a result as well?

Perhaps we could take a moment to look at two options: 1. Are we treating the symptom instead of the issue? And 2. Do we have examples in other countries we might be wise to consider?

First of all, the drinking age has not been established by the scientific or medical community determining the effects of alcohol in developing children, it has been established by motor vehicle accidents. Should we perhaps consider that our laws regarding the punishments for driving under the influence are where we should have targeted our energy? Is it also possible, that by making alcohol a rite of passage by legislating ages for consumption we are making alcohol more of a line of demarcation? Creating the illusions that consumption of alcohol is a sacrament by which one proves they are an adult. A bat mitzvah of sorts.

Do we have examples of other countries in which things are done differently?

I would point to Switzerland. (I would point there because my neighbor's grandson is from there and I spent a week talking about their drinking laws with him.)

At his age: 17 he has been legally able to drink for years, but still is not able to legally drive. There is no legal 'drinking age' in Switzerland. The age at which you can purchase alcohol is 16, but the age at which he can drive is 18. And the punishments for any alcohol at all while driving... (even a sip of cough syrup can throw a person over the breathalyzer), are incredibly severe. So, a young person learns first how to drink in moderation... then how to drive, and everyone in the country is paranoid about getting behind the wheel with even a bit of alcohol in their system. I think there is a good logic to this.

Can I see potential drawbacks to their system? Yes. Too restrictive.

I think kids who start driving at an earlier age tend to be better drivers... but, like many of you, having grown up here (in Crawford), kids began driving around the ranch when they were nine. (Yes, to the transplants from the city... I do mean nine.) But, most people do not live on seventy acres where a kid can tool around in a Jeep without any worry. Even still, I think getting kids out on dirt bikes and vehicles at a younger age makes for a superior driver, and to wait until they are eighteen seems excessive.

If anything, I think we likely coddle kids too long, keeping them from exercising the self-control and responsibility that is necessary to become a functional adult.

Now, don't misunderstand, I recognize that this coddling arises from a good place. Child labor, unfit parents, drunk driving accidents, there are a lot of kids who need more support than they get at home. Numerous issues have caused the government to step up and create regulations to protect kids from situations in which they were (and often still are) in harm's way. That said, to grow into a functioning healthy adult you have to start taking responsibility for your life, and the sooner those muscles are exercised they stronger they will be. And that is the ultimate goal, is it not?

Then again, perhaps we are looking at it all wrong? Perhaps the drinking age should be raised. If twenty-one is better... why not twenty-two? Why not thirty-two? And honestly, what ever happened to prohibition? I bet a lot of lives were saved! Perhaps we should make a new law. A good one! After all, if it saves just one life...

YOUR HEART NEEDS A HUG

Hug therapy is a thing now... and I'm giving it two big thumbs up! The necessity of physical contact has been scientifically proven. A child who is fed and taught but not given physical contact will languish. There have been heartbreaking animal studies in which chimpanzee babies were given their physical necessities but not love and snuggles.

It didn't go well.

These studies quickly demonstrated tremendous mental and physical damage to chimps who'd had their physical needs met, but zero emotional support. In further studies, if given the option, these little chimp babies would take abusive relationships if it came with comfort at times and would avoid a robotic, but perfectly safe environment. I think even discussing these studies is horrible, but that is how instinctive our understanding is that innocent little creatures need love and nurturing. When newborn babies are in ICU skin to skin snuggles are a matter of life and death. Those who work with these tiny, vulnerable humans find the use of skin to skin contact is invaluable. Adults need it as well – including you.

As soon as you hug you begin a cascade of hormonal responses. Your stress hormones decrease, the hormone oxytocin which is responsible for love and bonding is released and soon your blood pressure drops. This even happens if you look at a cuddly image – but it's stronger when you get in a cuddle yourself.

Not a snuggler? That's ok – a cat works as well, and they aren't big snugglers either. Even a small amount of physical connection with a pet will be helpful; as long as you are getting physical loving touches in your life on a consistent regular basis. Much like a pill – take this medicine several times per day. And how nice to realize that hugs are also a gift you can give. Just as giving hugs will perk up your health and strengthen your heart - you will be giving those benefits to anyone you hug.

Now, let us not take the cynical path of assuming that hugs are just an evolutionary construct that forces us to bond with our peers thereby causing us to behave as a creature more akin to ants than alligators. This may be grounded in truth, but it is also a miserable way to perceive the good of hugging.

Hey, imagine if you will the joyless experience of forcing oneself to hug as a cynic only interested in a hug for the perfunctory health benefits in which you recognized them to simply be a chemical reaction upon your nervous system. I suppose a hug may still feel a bit good... but I think it would lose its value immeasurably under such circumstances.

Let us instead take the more mystical vision. The Namaste' Hindu concept. The divine in me greets the divine in you. A hug is really at its best when you squeeze your heart right up to that person and press all the love you can from your heart into them. Give a big, big squeeze and hold your breath – maybe press your cheek to theirs... and release. That's a good hug! Purely magical – full of hope and shared bond. Convinced that your soul told their soul "wassup!" in the clearest way. Boom.

And then let all those happy chemicals fall all over you. A healthier stronger heart has been gained by both!

BEE-UTIFUL SOLUTION

Poor advice...

From what I have read, I am about to provide you with some terrible advice. My Facebook feed is currently filled with people begging for advice on how to deal with seasonal allergies, desperate for answers and I am ready to lay out a brilliant solution out for you... but – as I say, my google search swears that I should not give this advice. I am not coming at you from a place of great standing.

I read a recent article in Prevention Magazine that declared my personal solution to be completely lacking in evidence, and likely useless. I read that it is the least well researched and most dubious remedy for allergies of any the author could find. I read several intellectually sound researchers that pointed out that there were ZERO peer reviewed studies showing any efficacy for this treatment and its success...

But while you're asking... there are some pharmaceuticals that ARE well researched and only have a few side effects! (Long list of quickly spoken, scary, possible side effects – including, but not limited to: blindness, coma and death.) That's a joke... kind of.

So, my advice - that is poorly researched, on dubious scientific standing and with zero merit is this: Raw local honey will cure your allergies.

I base my knowledge on my personal experience... and my brother-in-law Ernie. And a guy from a climbing gym in California who's name I can't remember.

My last few years of high-school I got a "cold" in the spring. It was annoying. A doctor eventually pointed out that I didn't have a cold, I had allergies. They weren't bad, just some sneezing. Over the years they got worse and I began taking over the counter medications. Benadryl at first, followed later by stronger stuff. The medications slowly seemed less and less effective, and I spent spring more and more drowsy and dried out and miserable.

The guy in the climbing gym (Hangar 18 - in roughly 2001) mentioned that I should take honey for my allergies. He was a dirt-bag climber, and I was broke and raw honey was expensive – so that was the end of that. By 2006 I had to give up contact lenses and wear glasses from mid-April to early June because my eyes were so red, puffy and inflamed. I couldn't breathe. I had reached a point where there was nothing I could take without a prescription that helped. I was looking at paying for doctor's visits and expensive medications. We were still on a tight budget, with limited insurance and I couldn't fathom paying for that. I was pretty desperate and looking for another option. That's when I had a chat with my brother-in-law and he said that he was told to try raw local honey. He had put it in is coffee every morning and he didn't have any allergies any more. In fact, he wasn't even taking honey anymore and it had been years since they'd bothered him.

That convinced me. I found a bee-keeper in Montrose and started having tea with honey every single day. The next spring, I still had allergies but they were very mild... I could wear contacts and I was fine using over the counter stuff. The next spring, I had spent another year of taking a teaspoon per day of local honey. I didn't have to take a single allergy pill that year. Not one.

It's not scientific – it's not peer reviewed- but I have a religious zeal in my belief that raw local honey is a cure for seasonal allergies. I am sure some of you will recall my story of insane-shrieking-crazy-bee stings? That story exists because my devotion to honey lead me to raising bees for my own honey.

Don't get me wrong. I completely understand that any one person's experience is not a great way to make medical decisions. If I stub my toe and get rid of a headache the two would have nothing to do with one another. Correlation does not equal causation... especially when the sample size is one... (plus Ernie and some climber). So, I really do get that any one anecdotal situation is not evidence that demands a verdict. But, much like a personal spiritual experience, once you've had it, you're pretty certain that you're onto something. And if my Facebook feed is any indication, there are a whole lot of you who are ready for a revival.

*Raw honey should not be given to babies.

SAFETY FIRST...ISH

As snow is fast approaching I thought it wise to remind you that you are a cautious adult - always determined to use prudence and moderation in making important life choices; and that this is true – even when it comes to the activities of winter.

(I know you doubt me.) You wild Colorado natives! "Safety first?" you laugh, "Ha!" Winter is for the bold! You are a wild and crazy adrenaline junky! You are currently checking the skies. Anxious for those little white flurries to begin sticking to the earth. Ready to throw your feet into a couple slippery slivers of fiberglass and launch yourself off the top of a mountain. You will stare with a defiant look in your eyes as the delight, and trepidation of a triple black diamond run wizzes past you at forty miles per hour. You are downright adventurous! – Evil Keneivel was just a warm up act compared to the tricks you will pull in that park!

And that's just the beginning - what about sledding with your family! Wild people who wake up to snow drifts, toss babies and whatnot in the back of a car and careen up into the mountains. Never mind that you are driving on threadbare summer tires… who cares that you haven't a descent sled- (just inflate the old river tubes). No one cares if the children are wrapped up in fancy-shmancy gortex windbreaker non-sense – throw some Walmart grocery bags on over their tennis shoes and they'll be fine!!! That's right, a campfire in a barrel and a thermos full of cocoa. No one's slowing down for safety check or helmets! We'll get a snowmobile to pull the kids around until their eyelashes get frozen shut.

And then there's your truly great adventures. A few of you are so very bold – so shockingly crazy that these people are a mockery to your awesome adventurous soul. You are the magi of the mountains – the true ancient spiritual wanderers of the land… that's right – you are going back country split boarding. You will wander the forgotten trails high in the dry chapped winds. You are not risking a broken bone or a car accident. This is bigger than that. You are risking avalanche dangers… folks may never make it home. You are a bold – wild spirit. When they ask your purpose… you let your gaze grow soft and whisper the immortal words of Hillary… "Because it is there…"

So many flavors – you wild, adventurous Coloradans… ready to throw yourselves heedlessly onto Red Mountain pass without an ounce of fear, to cross country ski, snowshoe and ice climb – for fun. A spirit that has no fear, knows no bounds, looks at yards of black ice at 2 am… and shrugs.

You are not a 'safety first' people! You are not worried a bit!

But… allas… I am confident that you are. Safety is of great importance to you, I can prove it.

Did you know that every winter over 700 people will suffer a heart attack while shoveling snow? Yep.

Right??? That's just silly.

Nobody needs to take risks like that!

SMOKE DETECTORS AND SOCIAL MEDIA

"It is a truth, universally acknowledged... that when a smoke alarm battery dies, it will be during the middle of the night." Vanessa Hutton

This was a Facebook post from a friend of mine. Tell my it didn't make you grin. Not in schadenfreude... not that you loved the thought of her miserable night spent looking for the stupid alarm that's going off... No- it made you smile because after a miserable night, she made a joke about the annoying reality we all can relate to.

That's because she's hilarious and fun and awesome. She's also one of my very best friends. She is one of my very best friends because she is hilarious and funny and awesome. (It's the best kind of circular reasoning.)

It has been said that every life is either a tragedy or a comedy – the difference has less to do with the details than it does with how you present them. Let's examine how many other folks would have written this on social media:

"A miserable night and no sleep since my smoke alarm decided to run out of batteries at 3 am! (Angry face emoticon)"

Or perhaps this always intentionally vague post - sure to get you some attention: "Fine! I'll just accept that the universe HATES me!!!!" (This is always followed by angsty messages from her distraught friends trying to decipher what horrible situation has besought our victim.)

Or, maybe one of these: "Those who truly care about me will understand my pain (and share my status and a link to my online store...) I know who cares and who will..." Passive aggressive manipulation is so much more entertaining when it is written out!

Gotta love it! But my friend is my friend because even though she is a single mom, with two teenagers, who has faced her share of struggles, when faced with a night spent wandering bleary eyed from room to room searching for that dang smoke detector, she didn't feel sorry for herself – nope – she wanted to give people a laugh.

You know what's even more awesome? As a believer that suffering is a valuable and important part of the human experience I could easily argue that, with her lighthearted attitude my friend was diminishing the good work suffering produces. That invention, and creative problem solving are the birthright bestowed upon those in discomfort. The wheel wasn't invented because we were all stoked using our feet to move stuff.

But, I argue the opposite, a humorous attitude increases creative thought, or at the least, in no way diminishes the process. Soon my friend had comments on the need for a better option for the smoke detector to notify one that the batter was getting low. There were suggestions for a less ear-splitting tone so you could actually find the source of the noise, suggestions for a warning light that made the offending batter easier to locate. Mentions of higher end detectors that have resolved some issues, and discussions as to why the price point was untenable.

Who knows? A year from now some fine person who was engaged in that discussion may have solved the issues and we may all be using a whole new system for fire detection.

But, we will have lost a funny, common anecdote that we all once related to. It is strange how so many common issues have disappeared these days. Much like the desperation felt as a pay phone informed you that you were out of time... or having to listen through a song you didn't like on radio... Or the worst! Remember when you had a question and there was no way to just google the answer?

You just didn't know.

And maybe a friend would say they heard that blah blah blah... and that was the most authority anyone had on the truth? Ah... the bygone amusing situations that modernity has solved. Someday soon the smoke detector battery going off at 3 am – blasting intermittently so by the time you move toward a detector it has shut off... and at such a mind pounding decibel as to make it impossible to locate the source, that too will be an amusing memory of a bygone era. But for today – a funny note to make me smile on a Wednesday morning. And a lesson in wisdom on social media.

HERE COMES THE SUN

"Here comes the sun little darling – here comes the sun and I said... it's all right."
The Beatles

The sun has just shown up, and the people there have never been so grateful for the warmth, and beauty of these rays of sunshine. No people have ever been more grateful for a glimpse of sunshine than they are today in Houston Texas.

Houston is a place that sees far too much sun and far too little rain, as a general rule. A place where the complaints tend to be focused around heat, and drought and not enough water for the lawns they so desire. But not today. Today the lawns are gone... lying under floodwaters so vast and deep that the entire country is shocked staring in aw; highways obliterated, communities buried.

But, already we are watching the beauty of human compassion and perseverance. Neighbors and volunteers getting in and helping. This is when we see ourselves at our best. Our political climate has never been more divisive and destructive. We find ourselves getting sorted into camps. Us and The Others and no one better dare to step anywhere in the middle! There is no respect for those who think differently – only shame and condescension for The Other. After all -I can't stand all of you who disagree with me! Clearly, I'm right, so you must be dumb! So dumb... as to think I'm dumb... for thinking you're dumb!! I'm going to break into all caps soon... and tell you to defriend me if you're one of the dumb people who thinks I'm a dumb person!!

But – we got a break for a bit. There was an eclipse and we all looked up and agreed... this sun playing peekaboo with the moon... that was really cool. Whether you voted for the rich, connected, corrupt, lady or the rich, connected, corrupt, guy – we all agreed on the sun's eclipse. And we quit talking about who actually is dumb, just for a bit, and then Houston got soaked. People were still trying to go back to talking about who is worse... but we were just so worried about Houston we didn't have time to get mad. And we looked up again... at the rain... looking up – waiting for the sun – playing peekaboo with the rain clouds. Neighbors were saving neighbors. Volunteers from states all around began pouring in. We remembered that those dummies we can't stand are also kind and hardworking and ready to risk themselves to help others. We looked up... and the sun finally peaked out from behind the clouds.

The sun brings warmth, and hope, and help. The sun will dry out the land, bring light to the darkness and grow the new plants... And maybe, just maybe the sun will help us to ignore those cold, angry bitter voices hell bent on splitting us into Us and The Others, and maybe we will ignore the people who profit from keeping us focused on hating each other... and instead we will look up together and find common ground.

We can all agree on something. That sun is really good news right now. That sun is needed and wanted. Let's start with that. Let's agree on this one thing together. And maybe tomorrow... we can find something else to share.

THE THING YOU MEAN?

Words mean things... or do they?

Can I get you something?? Anything?? Nothing?? It's no big thing...

I know a thing or two... about that word... Thing.

Today if I mention the word, "thing," you assume a generic noun. I could mean a toy, or pen, or zucchini, or child. Whatever. A thing. Something – that for whatever reason – we are referencing without too great a specificity. But – that is not the original meaning of the word. Thing was once and illustrious and important word. A great and valuable thing.

A "Thing" originated as an assembly – more specifically as an early Germanic democratic parliament. (Cold, blond people discussing the political needs of the day.) The first mention of Things was an Icelandic thing.

Literally: An Icelandic Thing.

The Thing was important. Such an important thing that the king of Sweden Olof Skötkonung (980-1022) once recognized the Thing to be of greater authority than was he. A thing of great importance! On an interesting side note, the place where these Germanic peoples held their Thing was called a "Thingstead." Like a homestead... but for a thing.

How did the thing devolve from its illustrious and specific meaning to the bland and broad word of today?

I don't know. Wikipedia won't tell me... and do to the lazy research requirements of the present day, I figure - if it won't show up in the first page of a Google search, then it cannot possibly be found. However, let us imagine...

Perhaps a thing was soon somewhere you were going. Example: Where are you going? To "the Thing."

And then the Thing became less lauded as politics became embittered and dirty.

I know this sounds untoward and far from likely, but, I assure you, politics can often be contentious and ugly... historically. Obviously, we are far too civilized today – but there was a time when politics was so contentious that people may even just write off everyone who didn't agree with them. Isn't that funny?

So, historically speaking, perhaps it became a bit of an insult. For example – Person A: 'Sven is having a party!' Person B: 'No one wants to go to that thing.'

(See, Sven was part of the 'Raiding and Pillaging' political persuasion... obviously the 'Burning the Dead at Sea' political group was the superior of the Viking parties... *eye-roll...* I cannot stand those Pillaging Party losers.)

And from there I suppose it could simply refer to anything of so little value to be unworthy of a pronoun... Just any old thing.

And today – it carries such value in its description of non-value. It's both nothing... and everything. Anything can be something. If you 'do your thing,' are you doing a Thing? (Probably not.)

Thing is so necessary in describing all things, it's difficult to imagine speaking without it.

I am told that words mean things. Do they? For the very word that means 'thing' – no longer means the thing that thing should mean. So what thing, specifically, do words mean?

EXERCISE

This month I have been informed our paper intends to focus on exercise. It may surprise you to find that I am, what you might call, an exercise expert. I am super into fitness and such. Ok... maybe I am exaggerating a bit, or at least misrepresenting my qualifications. I suppose a better title would be that I am more of an exercise browser. A pursuer of all things fitness.

And I would venture to say most Americans fall into this camp. I know some genuine, decade long running enthusiasts. But, I know a lot more people who have bought the special shoes and spandex and reflective outfits, trained for a 5k and then for a half marathon and then put the shoes up never to run much again.

We all do this. It's not really a bad thing. We have a million interesting exercise possibilities why limit ourselves to just one? That would be downright un-American! We must explore the world of exercise! Embrace the possibilities. Thai chi with a little road biking, a touch of gym rat body pump and a sprinkle of Zumba. It's just how we roll.

I've done a lot of different programs. Years of CrossFit,

Gold's classes, lots of free weights, rock climbing, and dancing. But you will find one area of exercise is a yawning void in my repertoire: anything aerobic. I mean... that stuff is horrible!

I am already on record as being against aerobics. You remember that right? If your face is red and flushed, your breathing rapid and your heart rate skyrocketing... something is WRONG! That's a sign of an allergic reaction. You should definitely stop!

I digress. But, I do have a current favorite exercise. It's called Yoga. I know you don't know what it is, but all the mommies walking around the school parking lot in stretchy tight pants that show... well...everything?? Yoga is the sport that you can thank for the outfit. Yoga pants – pajamas for everyday life. No, I'm not lazy – in fact, I'm working out!

It originated as a Hindu practice. (That's a religion – Hinduism. You know the people Columbus thought he found hanging out on our coasts? They often practice it.) I'm not personally a Hindu, but I did read the Bhagavad-Gita once... It's cool.

I LOVE yoga for a few reasons. Number one, I'm flexible. Not something I worked at much - just naturally the way I am – but in a Yoga class suddenly I look like I'm an expert with years of practice. It's nice to just walk in and be good. That hasn't happened much in my life- really ever.

THEN, I actually love the religious element. Forcing your body to suffer at the will of the soul. It's really cool to think about, and since thinking about theology is just about my favorite thing ever – it's a win/win. Again, I recognize this isn't something most people would normally enjoy. Most people would have to work hard to make themselves study ancient beliefs. I think it's fun the way normal people watch HGTV or sports or those Kardashian people... wait, I mean women... they're all women now, right?

Then there is Shavasana. This is the final pose in yoga.

Do you know what this is???? DO YOU?!?!?

Yoga ends with NAP TIME!!! You get to take a five minute nap and call it a workout! I AM NOT KIDDING. You have to do this. I think all workouts should end in nap time. Come on Kelly Brown! Naptime after Murph??? (This is a CrossFit joke, it's really not that funny if you didn't follow, so don't feel like you're missing out on anything.)

Yeah – so that's my best advice on exercise. Do all those weird hodgepodge of workouts that appeal to you... pole dancing with some aerial silks – a kickboxing class on Tuesdays, mountain biking Thursday. Most of us do it – and I'm fairly confident that the most important thing is to just keep moving... even if you never get passionate about any one thing.

But, if you're still experimenting a bit with your exercise repertoire– try some yoga. It's a flexy workout, with a hint of church and a nap. Perfect!

RAISING LITTLE GIRLS

My daughter has a mullet. This is not because we are bad parents. (Obviously any parent raising a kid with a mullet is not a good parent, this goes without saying.) Just kidding. Hairstyles do not define parenting, but, clearly, if your kid has a mullet, we are judging you.

So, here's the story: The mulletted one is so mulletted because she recently grabbed some scissors and chopped off the front half of her hair. We aren't really sure when it happened—which *does* prove that we are bad parents. And what doubles down on our terrible parenting? A small part of us admired her for doing it, because–Hey! That's some initiative!

She has also taken to wandering the house with a Nerf gun and yelling, "Suck it up Princess!" and then firing the suction cup 'bullets' at the nearest wall. She's tiny... pre-school. Her voice is too cute to be believed when she yells this.

I'm not certain where this desire to shoot princesses has come from. In our efforts to shelter and coddle our children in the traditional 'helicopter parenting' style of our Generation X parenting culture, we have no cable television. So, I am wondering what it was that she found on Netflix? What has SpongeBob been up to? And who are the evil ones?

Wolves often. No idea why that is either? What did a wolf ever do to her? She's afraid of wolves and wants to shoot princesses who need to 'suck it up.' Hmmmm...

I listen to her waging war around the house, ready to take on the evil doers. Perhaps I should intervene and ask her to kindly work out her differences with the evil ones; tell her to use her words, maybe encourage civil dialog with maturity?

But I don't.

Raising girls is a weird and difficult proposition. I'm fighting a society that tells her to value her looks above her thoughts, or to feign weakness for the sake of femininity. Yet, I recognize I am also required to help her function in a world where appearances really do matter, for all people, and where social skills actually are required.

Sure, yelling, "Suck it up Princess!" and shooting suction cups isn't generally an effective motivational technique as an adult (Unfortunately. I once tried it at a PTA meeting), but, whatever evil she is battling in the kitchen this afternoon, she is a strong, confident beast. She's kicking booty and taking names.

The world will do just fine covering many of the girly lessons. She's going to learn mascara tips and the art of giggling more than necessary from some Cosmo style women's magazine soon enough. Today, however, this girl is taking her mullet on parade and running the world! And, regardless of the pressures facing women in a postmodern world of blah blah blah, every woman since the beginning of time has needed to demand that someone suck it up... princess.

AND A TIME TO CURSE...

Fans of Doctor Richard Steven's research can now enjoy his latest book, "Black Sheep: The benefits of being bad." It expands upon his published research on pain and the benefits of swearing. He stated in a recent interview that his interest came when his wife was in labor. He found her using language that was 'less than cordial' and wondered why? And, like any good scientist facing the greatest day of his life, watching his wife in incredible pain, he began to wonder if there wasn't a research grant to be written?

Soon enough the study was set up and the protocol established. He created "non-damaging pain" using ice water and tested subjects in a control group by asking them to place their arms into the ice water and cope with the pain silently. He then had his experimental group cope while using curse words. It turned out that the people using foul language fared 50% better. With repeated experiments the results have held.

Think about that for a moment. Research proves that

cursing reduces pain. One would assume it was just a response to the pain, but in actuality, it is serving a purpose.

In follow-up experiments subjects for the control group were asked to use non-swear words in an effort to control the pain. It didn't work. It's gotta be the real deal. It was also discovered that if you are more creative and articulate in swearing – the effect is greater. Great news for all! If you are in pain – throw out a few swear words and you will cope a bit better —and hold on a bit longer.

Good to know.

But, there was a caveat that I feel is even more intriguing. If a person self-reported that they regularly used swear words they found the pain numbing to be less effective than those who didn't regularly swear.

This begs so many interesting questions!! Why is it that a word... any word -could help lessen pain? A word is just a word after all. What is it about the "naughty" words that makes them work? The answer seems to be that they are set aside as naughty. That we give them a certain significance by recognizing them as a talisman for something dark or dirty.

It evokes images of dark wizards and witchdoctors doesn't it? Incantations – words with power.

How can nonsense letters just piled together have that much strength? How do words that we disparage in polite company come to be medically beneficial? And why is it that if you throw profanity around on a day to day basis it loses its power?

Fascinating questions! The only way to get a real benefit from the naughty words is to actually treat them as if they are naughty. To make an effort to give them a special, sacred place in your life; 'The words that must not be named' if you will. Special, unacceptable words, which can come to your aid in a time of need.

...And if your husband is a research scientist can provide him with a source of income, which is good. Especially if you're in the worst pain of your life and he's being a total @*#&$*#&@!

MONEY WELL SPENT

Don't go to college. Just don't. It's a terrible idea. At least according to Wall street investor and all around interesting guy James Altucher.

Many of us were encouraged to go to college when we were young. Of course, we must invest in our education! After all, a person who attends college will make $17,500 more per year, on average, than a person who doesn't. In a lifetime that will equate to more than $2 million!! How could you not?

But, my dear friends, as a fan of economics I encourage you to embrace the beautiful phrase: 'Correlation does not equal causation'. Meaning, just because college education and higher income are correlated, does not mean that the education was the cause.

More to the point, people who go to college have many reasons to be more successful than those who do not. People who attend college – on average – will have a higher IQ than people who didn't, they will likely be more driven, and from a family in a higher economic bracket, and so able to draw from more resources. This demonstrates that there is already a strong selection bias for college students. And, with studies such as the Housing Voucher Program by the Center on Budget and Policy Priorities, we find that growing up in a situation in which you experienced a higher standard of living as a child generally equates a higher standard of living as an adult. (In other words: regardless of your IQ, your opportunities or any other metric, most people will seek out the standard of living they knew as a child - and achieve it.)

So, take the same person who would typically go to college: he has a decent GPA, his parents have socked away some money for his education, and instead of sending him to college, use the money to invest in a trade, or buying a rental property or even doing volunteer work and traveling; would that investment go farther for that student than if that same money had been used to help pay for college? Assuming that student pursued a high-income career that required a college degree perhaps not. (These would be examples such as Engineering, or Medicine.) But, if that degree is in something more esoteric, and ladens him with debt I bet so. It's hard to see how a twenty-year-old with a trade or an investment and no debt is in a worse position than his alter ego with tens of thousands in debt and a degree in European History.

All of this, to me, seems quite logical. Ditch the college path. It's gotten far, far too expensive. There are too many degree holders waiting tables (author waves hand – gestures to self).

However, it is important to recognize, that this is generally NOT the accepted common-sense position. Nearly every expert on the planet will disagree with Mr. Altucher on his theory. In fact, he has admitted that in spite of his notoriety for arguing vehemently against the value of a college education, when it comes to his children... they want to go to college.

GOING GREEN

For today's edition of Valley Health we are focusing on going green. The easiest way to "Go green" is with a food safe dye, (Bah-dum- *tis)

But it will not give you the sense of being a good citizen and steward of the planet that you are likely hoping to elicit. Assuming you wanted a less literal version, I have a few other tips that may accomplish the goal.

Mulching is a good way to go green... it's also a good way to get Centipedes, mice and a rather stinky pile of stuff behind your home. For this reason, I would recommend keeping the mulch far away from the house – maybe use your neighbor's home. This can be satisfying on several levels... It is cathartic to know that your scraps of food are not going to waste and with the condition of the soil around here (which is just the worst... is anyone else living on clay??? It's THE WORST!!) every single lawn clipping and coffee ground is helping make the dirt a little less horrible.

The downside of centipedes is a very important issue, however. I really hate centipedes. I feel sad when I kill a mouse... but not centipedes. They should die based solely on the nature of being a centipede. A centipede gives me the heebeegeebees in a way I cannot possibly communicate. I immediately feel like they are on my neck... and in my stomach... and I need to somehow crawl out of my skin in order to escape them. Ugh! So, while a mulch pile is awesome... you might need to get your teenager or husband or – really anyone, to help with the pile. Just to avoid the centipedes.

I also like growing your own fruits and vegetables as a healthy, environmentally friendly idea. Theoretically – I have yet to actually get a garden to grow. We have rabbits, deer, prairie dogs and squash bugs. These guys have eaten 90% of everything I have managed to grow. I have sprayed things with wolf urine smell... and all-natural pesticides and yet – so far – I am only theoretically a fan of having your own vegetable garden.

For my final going green tip I'd like to suggest getting bike, or a good set of walking shoes and using your two feet to get around town. Did you know that in China right now 90% of children are near sighted?? Ninety percent!!! For decades we were told that near sightedness was genetic (It's shocking how often experts tell us facts that turn out to be wrong. It would be awesome if, in the future, all expert statements began with "we think." For example: "We think" near sightedness is genetic, or "we think" fat free food is healthier, or "we think" gravity is really, really real.) (That last one was a joke... we think)

So, now that it is apparent that near sightedness is not genetic (or certainly not 100% genetic), the question is, what does cause near sightedness? And it appears that too much time indoors is the primary culprit. (It's theorized that too little bright sunlight, and too much looking at things near your face are the culprits.) So – my best tip for going green would be to get outside! Ride your bike to the store or walk to Wal-Mart. Get a wagon and go on foot to grab your groceries, like a European. It will keep the air cleaner, keep you in better shape, get you a helping of vitamin D and it's good for your eye-sight as well.

PINTEREST AND THE PROBLEM WITH YOUR DIET.

I think I can sum up your diet issues with one word. Pinterest.

Pinterest is a social media thingy that allows people to 'pin' the stuff they are interested in... the population of Pinterest is 98% female, and 90% of their pins fall into two distinct categories:

1. Recipes for dark, decadent, chocoholic, rich, super-indulgent, better-than-anything-ever-in-your-life cake... and
2. Dieting advice.

This is reality.

We all want to find the "sitting on the couch, watching Netflix and eating cookies diet." For some reason this diet never catches on...

Or actually – it catches on, but the results are... questionable.

I thought I'd put together a list of books I've bought in the name of health and fitness. We have Omnivore's

Dilemma... (It said we had to avoid corn... and any animal that ate corn... and anything made with corn syrup.) I also have Wheat Belly... I think it's clear what we avoid there. I have the Blue Zone diet, the Mediterranean diet, Ayurvedic diets and Daniel diets. And fitness books: Born to Run, Supple Leopard, lots of Yoga books and honestly hundreds – hundreds of rock climbing books.

I should be an expert! Look at the education I have gained! But, all that reading and I'm not an expert. Lots of people are trying diets and finding they aren't working. We are all highly educated un-experts.

Side note: If you Wikipedia Zooey Deschanel – I am not kidding – it says that she was allergic to eggs, and dairy and wheat and was Vegan!!! Do you understand what that means???? She could eat... like... air and water and carrots. It says she just recently had to abandon her diet because it wasn't working out well. You think? I may not have as healthy a diet as she does... but I think I might be a bit superior in another area. (Wink wink) Right?! (Do you see what I did there? I'm implying that I'm smarter than her... it's funny.)

So, we should be vegetarian or vegan? I think if we did we'd need to eat a lot of grains – which are now terrible! We have now learned that those grains made us all fat - and sick - and according to the Paleo people who are vegan-ish (but with yes to eating animals but no to peanuts) grains are a travesty unleashed upon mankind! So, no grains for Paleo's and Atkin's – But, yes grains to vegetarians and vegans but only for "good grains."

But, what are the good grains? We know now that we shouldn't eat wheat, or corn... so maybe rice? Rice! But not white rice! No white things!

White is bad! Unless you're eating sushi... then suddenly it's totally cool.

White potatoes, white rice, white bread... white...??

What?

Too soon? Are we still pretending there isn't another unacceptable white thing?

But, how are vegetarian diets supposed to work if we aren't eating any grains... especially processed ones? Everyone live on quinoa? Is that a grain?

Makes the argument for being vegetarian difficult. I mean, it's hard to not die if you're a vegetarian who doesn't eat grains.

Then others argue vegetarians are dead wrong! After all, the Tigers and Wolves and Sharks aren't trying it out... and maybe Mother Nature understands the whole "circle of life - predator and prey" a bit better than we do.

Mufasa seemed to have it handled. Although Simba became some sort of insectitarian? Right?

Could we just take a moment and think of all the stinking kids movies premised on carnivores becoming vegetarians? Finding Nemo – Shark tale – The Lion King – Madagascar... and 2... and 3... and the Christmas special... Zootopia... I am sure I've forgotten some. I just can't see how the carnivore becomes vegetarian theme can go on any longer? Can the Mommies and Daddies of the planet unite and say we'd like the children's movie producers to find a new theme??

... Finding Dory...

Assuming Mufasa was right and all other Disney and DreamWorks storylines are false, it may not be a terrible idea to assume that Mother Nature's got the predator-prey thing going for a reason, and not fight nature quite so hard.

But, again... where would that leave us? Still highly educated in a lot of great ideas... that don't really work...

I don't see that any one person has found the perfect diet. I think it's likely because we are all so stinking drawn to the cookies and TV plan. It's such a FUN plan!

I supposed – when it comes to diets – that's the way it's going to be. They suck, and they're hard, and working out isn't a lot of fun. But – being fit and healthy is worth the trouble. Kinda...

I'm going to go now – I need to Pin a recipe for a cake made with double the fat – triple the sugar and you substitute Dr. Pepper for the water! (Don't roll your eyes... it's a thing.)

PLAYING IN THE WATER

I AM A TERRIBLE SWIMMER. I MEAN, I CAN DOGGY paddle like a beast, but... from the odd expressions it's clear that many of you are less than impressed with that skill. I also am one of those people who acts like a total baby when getting into a swimming pool. I know that the proper, socially accepted mode of entrance is a cannon ball. But, I don't ever seem to have the courage for it. I do that lame mom-waddle, shudder, flinch from stair to stair as I enter the chronically too cold pool water.

But, in spite of my cat like reflexes when approaching all swimming pool activities, I do still love playing in water. I am quite fond of our annual visits to Lake Powell. I have learned to water ski and surf the wake... sort of. I'm a bit squatty looking in the videos... and my expression comes across as pained for some reason. But, I do have fun. And, I will admit, I have in fact, bruised my entire backside trying to be cool jumping off the cliffs like my children. Yes, I did spend the next several days standing. And yes, everyone did look at my rear end and then gasp, and then exchange worried/bemused glances over my head. But still, I think on the whole it was fine. Pretty sure I came across like one of those outdoorsy moms they plaster all over Athleta magazines.

And, I have demonstrated my keen water abilities when trying my hand at rafting the Gunnison with my husband. It was fun, and fairly uneventful. With exception to the time I managed to launch a good ten feet when our raft went sideways on a rock. I did decide that I was going to die for a time, as I kept not surfacing... and not surfacing... and not surfacing. When I did finally surface (whew!) I was fine. I may have wrapped my quivering legs around a rock and hung there desperately refusing to move... until a 10-year-old in a kayak came and rescued me. But, that's really the logical response when you have been pretty sure you were going to die. The ten-year-old was very kind. He spoke to me in soothing tones that assured me I was in no way to feel ashamed... I would be just fine.

So, I think it's clear that while I may not have the prowess in water sports that many of you possess, I am still a fan. You will find me at river bottom water park this summer. Nervous, sure, but I intend to go down the river a few times. And I do imagine you will find me at the Rec Center, hopefully just lounging on the side, but I'll make a few trips with my kids down the slide.

And there's always Ouray; sitting in hot water and not moving a muscle. The truth is, that's the water of my people. No shuddery waddle into a cold pool... no cardio, or life risks... and you're always welcome to join us too. No cannon balls.

KIND OF HIGH MAINTENANCE

Gluten allergies are not funny. It's heartbreaking to watch a child have to pass on birthday cake and cookies and many of the fun things their friends are enjoying.

This column is about something kind of funny. It's not people who have allergies, and it's not people who have religious and moral convictions about the foods they eat. Ok? Everyone knows what is not funny... what we aren't allowed to mock.

Can we admit though, that some stuff might be funny?

You know... the diets of the high maintenance people.

The people who are gluten free 'just because' and don't even know what gluten is. (Carb? Protein? Fat??) People who are vegan because they love animals while they own cars with leather seats. The people who 'can't' eat lettuce because they have an 'allergy' and for the life of you, you cannot recall lettuce allergies. Google it – apparently, it's a thing.

I once spent an afternoon with a college friend who NEEDED watermelon juice. I'm not kidding. She didn't want it – it was a need. Her boyfriend had to spend four hours in traffic while they drove around to fancy-shmancy juice shops looking for watermelon juice. It didn't work out. (Not the juice, they found that. The relationship.)

In CrossFit land they like Paleo: I can drink my milk whole (YES!!) and pound the bacon and avocados and never have to watch my calories! Except – Peanut butter is evil. Because??? Because back when humans were still half ape we didn't eat peanuts so there is a moral imperative to avoid peanuts.

Did you get that? All things being equal peanuts are a fairly healthy food... but because the hunter gatherers didn't eat them... I can't? I have to ask... how do we know they didn't? I bet I could get an ape to eat a peanut. If I could- then could I eat them? Did hunter gatherers not bump into peanuts? Were they not smart enough to shell them? Are thumbs too important? –apes have thumbs too. I'm pretty sure we are guessing here.

Or then there's the vegetarian and vegan diets. I would like to have the compassion necessary to embrace this. They seem so much more appealing as a moral system. I mean – they're kind to animals! But... but so many vegetarians like to wear leather shoes.

Because - leather shoes are awesome! And so are leather couches! Love them! And 7th day Adventists have incredibly high life expectancy and they are often vegetarians. But... recent studies have found that if you take the 7th day Adventist out of the equation (they also benefit from close knit community of faith) vegetarians actually have the same life expectancy as meat eaters... and they have higher rates of depression. Probably because it's really depressing to not eat bacon. I mean... bacon.

Then, there are the Atkins people. They can't have

anything BUT meat and cheese. So that's a good way to get burned out on bacon really fast. I bet two days in you want a salad sooooooooo bad!

Or there's the no carb people: they have to walk by the enticing aroma of baked goods. Not like how a gluten free person can't eat wheat but can have cupcakes from rice flour. People who don't eat carbs can't have any baked goods, or potatoes, or corn, or happiness.

Some people don't like dairy, because milk turns calves into cows... so what's it going to do to you? They look at you when they say this, as though the logic is so obvious. They are intensely fearful for your wellbeing... Clearly you are just six months away from becoming a cow!!! Except humans have been consuming dairy for as long as we have walked upright... and... you know... if it ain't broke. Plus - I mean cheese??? Some stuff is worth the damage. (By stuff I meant cheese.)

I heard that Steve Jobs tried out being a fruitarian. Have you heard of this? According to the excellent authority I found (on Wikipedia), Job's fruitarian interests were the inspiration for Apple... the company... its name... because apples are fruit.

Fruitarians believe we should only eat fruit. This is so nothing ever dies on behalf of your desire to eat. Including plants. For example, a carrot was living until you harvest it. So, you killed it. But fruit will fall off of the tree anyway, which means you are allowed to kill the apple for your sustenance. I heard Jobs could be a real jerk though. Maybe a carrot or two might have mellowed him out? Or... bacon. Mmmmmm... But, you know, baby steps.

My personal favorite? The "eat local" movement; I like that one. Local foods if you live in downtown LA are like - cockroaches, ants, and ice plant. But in Montrose??

Venison, corn, fruit, honey, veggies, chickens, fish, beef. I mean – how awesome is that?

With the eat local movement I can look down on city people (I was doing it anyway) and act pretentious and judgmental because they are destroying the environment by hauling food all over the planet in order to eat in their concrete jungle. I will remind them of their horrible carbon footprint and their wasteful choices. I will be so meaningful and self-righteous! I can't wait.

Until I want orange juice. Or guacamole. Or a banana. Did I say Guacamole? I will NOT give up on guacamole! Life is too short. And guacamole needs lime and salt! None of those are local! Whatever would I do?

The self-righteous judgement opportunity isn't worth it. I want to eat all sorts of yummy foods and not eliminate some big swaths of food. I don't have any allergies, and heck – isn't that the benefit of being a Protestant? We almost never have to sacrifice anything! It's the glutton's religion. Saint Peter had a dream and I get to eat Lobster because of it! Woohooo!!

Just kidding. If we are bagging on diets – the Twinkies and Pepsi and tobacco diet, because: "I do what I want," is likely going to end badly too.

So, I'm proposing the self-control and good judgment diet. It works well, and not just for food. It works well for business choices, relationship advice, and moral dilemmas. It's never going to become a new trendy fad and catch on in a big way and you rarely get to be condescending, because your choices vary constantly based on the circumstances. It can be difficult, but everything has its sacrifices.

EAT THE PUMPKIN PIE.

Life is about balance. On balance... if you are over 25 you should probably be working out most every day of the week, you should also eat a salad for dinner and fruit for breakfast. You notice I didn't say a salad WITH dinner... I said a salad FOR dinner.

You don't have to, you can eat Twinkies for dinner, you're a grown up. But, don't complain about your thighs to me. If you see an adult who is fit and healthy, then I promise you they are eating a lot more broccoli than they want to and doing push-ups when they'd rather sit on the couch.

Hey, we all are hoping to find the cheesecake and Barcalounger diet. Seriously. Sign me up now. But... it doesn't exist. Dinner tonight? Salad with chicken. Tomorrow- salad with Salmon. The next day? Salad. That's life. That's how it's going to look.

But the holidays are coming up now. How are we going to survive on our diets for the holidays? We aren't. That's how.

Thanksgiving is one day. One. Eat the turkey and gravy and pumpkin pie. Christmas will have a handful of family meals or office parties. Go ahead and eat. That's what a celebration is. It's a day in which you step outside of your normal behavior. Don't bother with healthy eating on Christmas. It's a day for celebrations. You go big. They are supposed to be special – you don't get that many. How you eat this holiday…? I don't think you should stress too awful much about it. What you need to be worrying about is what you're doing on all the other days. I'll tell you what you're doing. You're eating salad. That's what. You're going to Golds, or CrossFit, or whatever your particular torture is and making yourself hurt. It's not for fun. It's because that's how life is. You earn your Christmas meals. And then. You eat that pumpkin pie and appreciate this celebration. You won't have a many in your life. And with the healthy way you eat on the rest of the days… hopefully you'll get a few more.

COME OUT SMELLING LIKE A ROSE

I'M NOT SAYING THAT I'M COMPLETELY STRESSED OUT planning the Dancing with the Stars fundraiser for this weekend... but if I were... I might be tempted to phone in this column. And if I was a total stress case as I tried to get this amazing fundraiser pulled together (benefits ten local charities - youshouldtotallygo) then I might get it in my head that I could use this column to do a quick product review for something I have become addicted to. So, assuming that perhaps this fundraiser on Saturday has, in fact, created some time constraints, I will go ahead and tell you about the product I recently discovered that is so impressive - it's worthy of a column.

Schmidt's hippie deodorant! You know what I mean by hippie deodorant? Those deodorants you find in the healthy granola stores, the weird crystals and herbal shmeers, the kind that never-ever works and leaves all our Telluride friends smelling of more than aroma of marijuana that generally perfumes their essence. Telluride scent: Parfum de Body Oder with a hint of Chronic (that's marijuana humor... at least I think so.)

But, now – for those of us, hippie or otherwise, who are interested in avoiding synthetic chemicals shmeared on our skin – there is an option that I SWEAR really, truly works.

It's called "Shmidts," and, unfortunately, it's a bit pricey. That's the downside... and after purchasing the Rose-Vanilla scent I can say for certain that you should NOT buy the Rose-Vanilla. But the Cedar wood Juniper smells wonderful and, I am not making this up, it works. It works incredibly well. It works better than any deodorant I've ever purchased – hippie or normal, including those maximum-extreme-ultra-mega versions. I do not know if it works better than a prescription – I've never taken my deodorant needs to that level. But, this is good enough that I have found myself forgetting that I need deodorant. I have gone up to two days with one application and managed to smell amazing the whole time. I know it's unusual for me to use this column to sing the praises of a product, but this stuff truly is impressive. And this is my thinking here... #1 – this is an opinion column... and this is my opinion... right? And #2 I think that just as Telluride has its distinct aroma... we could invent the Parfum de Montrose and it would be that we are – like – never stinky! That seems like a winner to me!

So, for all of you who like getting a good Twyla hug now and then- you're welcome. I shall henceforth be a more pleasant hug... even after yoga. And, if you're in the market for some hippie deodorant, and don't mind spending a bit more if it works really well... then this stuff is for you.

VIDEO GAMES

Video games will rot your brain. I don't have to prove this, we've all seen the carnage. The pale, clammy, millennials living in their parents' basements as they plug themselves into a void of guns, violence and disturbing time-suck. Endless streams of greasy food, wasted lives, and no vitamin D. That's the cliché... we've all met one. What good could possibly come from those games?

Except... I suppose there is some problem solving. I mean, how else would a person win a complicated video game? Problem solving skills must be developed in order to win. They do win right? (It seems like there are several games that aren't really games). Like Minecraft, my kids never win that game, it's more like fancy-shmancy Legos. Isn't it?

Actually, there is another reason to support the video game lover in your life. There is some evidence that video games may actually be very useful – to the right person, in the right context.

If – for example – you could think of a real-life career in which the techniques of a video game could translate to skills necessary for real life... we might have to take our cliché, judgmental attitudes and shelve them for a more open-minded view.

And there is. (A job where you regularly work in a virtual world to accomplish a difficult technical skill in the actual world.) A job where the hand eye coordination at a very fine level was incredibly important. Have you figured it out? What career has been positively impacted by the joy of video gaming?

Surgery – laparoscopic surgery to be exact.

A 2007 study in the Journal of the American Medical Association found that surgeons who had played video games at least 3 times in the past week had 37% fewer errors when they practiced performing laparoscopic surgery and they were 27% faster than their non-gaming counterparts. The study also asked surgeons to play video games to test how well a positive video game score correlated with a positive score on "Top Gun" laparoscopic surgical skills. To research the video to surgery correlation – they used Super Monkey Ball 2 as their first game.

I am not making this up.

There is a valid, useful, medical study in which surgeons played Super Monkey Ball 2... for science. They followed SMB2 with a game of Star Wars, Racer Revenge and then Silent Scope. And sure enough, playing the video games before performing the laparoscopic surgery did in fact increase success rates, and decrease times. The highest correlation was with Super Monkey Ball 2. If a surgeon had the high score on that game... she was likely the best surgeon as well.

So, when researching your next surgeon keep this study in mind. I recommend you interview a few surgeons, get different opinions. Ask them about their interests... maybe challenge them to a game of Super Monkey Ball 2. You're obviously in need of an intelligent, hardworking professional... but don't be afraid of the pasty millennial who spends too much time zoned out in front of a screen. He may just be your safest bet for an exceptional surgeon.

WEIGHT LOSS ADVICE

I know some of you have put on weight over the holidays. I'm not speaking from personal experience here. I didn't look at the scale yesterday and feel a little shiver of dread pour over me. But, some of you did.

In my time on earth, I have watched the scale do this on several occasions, so I will give you my best advice for pulling the scale down a few notches, but only based on my past experience, I am not currently facing this situation, because a woman in her forties doesn't keep making the same mistakes every holiday season – obviously. She knows better than to cave to her cravings when facing, say, a bourbon pecan pie. But, for you young folks who may have caved here's what I like to do:

#1 Intermittent fasting. Basically – I only eat one meal per day; and for me, it's great. Most cultures practice fasting, but in Western society we have worried it was dangerous or could even slow your metabolism long term, so we avoid it and look at our results!! (Laughing face emoticon)

Intermittent fasting has some great benefits. Autophagy

is a state your body enters while fasting, and it's a very healthy important time. It has been described by biologists as the "garbage disposal." When in autophagy your body begins to consume itself. That may sound creepy, but much of what is consumed is pre-cancerous cells. If you're interested, Scientific American has a great article online: "How Intermittent Fasting may help you live a longer and healthier life," which boils down a lot of the statistics.

And several doctors, among them Dr. Rhonda Patrick, are preaching the Intermittent fasting gospel far and wide.

#2 Eating apples. I have found I can always lose weight if I eat enough apples. If I eat one apple a day I maintain my weight, two apples per day I lose at least 1/3 a pound per day. Three apples and I lose almost one pound per day. It's very effective... it also makes you really hate apples. I did once try to eat apples and cheesecake all day... that didn't work. You can gain weight on cheesecake - no matter what. But, eating a normal diet plus apples is a weight loss miracle for me.

So, there you got it, my personal favorites. Hopefully most of you moved from Thanksgiving to New Years without adding an ounce of happy, comfort calories celebrating with friends and family. But, if you did dare to enjoy your life for a couple weeks without obsessing over your food – then you may want to try these diet tricks to help get back on track. Not me, of course.

SO, WHAT IS A SOUL?

"'Till he appeared and the soul felt it's worth..."
Oh Holy Night

CHRISTMAS! THE MASS FOR CHRIST... AN IDEA WHICH had me listening to carols about the soul discovering its worth, and begging the question... what do we mean by our souls? As a tremendous fan of apologetics, I love thinking about such things. And so, I thought, a dive in the deep end might be a fun Christmas column... So... What is a soul?

Some cultures discuss Chi, or a universal spirit... these are fun, awesome concepts; but today I wanted to focus on 'the reason for the season': the Judeo-Christian version of the soul. "I am." (How cool is that description?) It's the name of God – it's the essence of his being —"I am." Who is God? He is.

"I am." What are you? The child of - made in the image of: I am. We are. He is – you are.

These days, the most popular philosophy of reality is arguably Materialism. It's easy to understand why– it's tangible, visible, straight forward. I'm not typing on an, "I am." There's not some ethereal essence getting stuff done here. I'm not typing on love, or chi or chakras. I'm typing on plastic keys on a very real keyboard that puts my thoughts into a computer, shoots them into outer space via a combination of 1's and 0's, which will be shot back to the Montrose Press in a Word document, to be printed and physically delivered to you! It's awesome and feels almost magical, but it's all very real, very firmly material, and requires no illustrious visions of souls or magical beings to explain it.

The material world has fantastic, solid explanations... no need for souls... but there are a few small hiccups in the logic. I'll point out two... small – beautiful hick-ups.

The first all of that awesome material un-magical stuff. It came – not from robots, it came from ideas. Ideas are the true root source of all the cool stuff... and ideas – well, they are magical. For example – the zeros and ones that will be used to move my thoughts from my computer, to the Daily Press... it's all based on crazy math... the mathematic principals of quantum physics.

One of the primary principals in quantum physics... is the observer effect. Matter in this universe does not take a form until it has been observed. Before it is observed it exists... but in a cloud of possibility - a set of options. Then upon observation – it picks. (I know it seems insane.) But, I am not simply convoluting a very complex idea– this is true. At the heart of the physical world, existence is dependent on the "I am" noticing that "it is." Without the "I am" nothing would actually be... it would be "thinking" about being. It would stay a possibility...

Einstein famously grew frustrated with the bizarre physics coming from the world of quantum mechanics. This was when he discussed Schrodinger's cat. In fact, at one point Einstein declared that he'd, "like to believe that the moon exists whether or not I'm looking at it." You'd think he had a point there... but no. The moon doesn't exist if you didn't look at it.

That feels ridiculous, doesn't it? But, the math that proves that the moon needs someone to check it out, is the same math that will take this column, turn it into ones and zeros – shoot it to a satellite, back into Mr. Lindburghs' computer and print it up for you. There's not a more tangible, defensively proven science than the mathematical theorems we use to surf the internet or skype to our family from the other side of the planet. And that math – requires that matter is not fixed in reality... until we look.

Who looks? You do. I do. I am.

The second hick-up? Faith. Pharmaceutical giants struggle against it every day. They don't call it faith – they call it placebo... but potato-potahto. If I convince you that you will heal... there is much greater chance that you will heal, than if you did not believe. If I use fancier pills... or even better - inject you with needles, you are even more likely to heal - because I increased your faith. The stronger your faith – the higher the placebo effect.

How, in a material world, is faith so medically effective that a drug must prove to be more powerful than faith in order to demonstrate its efficacy? If the material world is all that is, then faith cannot be of any value... much less of significant value. Where is faith coming from? If the brain could have fired up the immune system to heal itself, why does it need faith in order to do so? Why should belief play any roll? What believes? A computer? A robot? Chemicals hopping across dendrites? Or... do I? Do you?

You are... I am.

Ah... the weird, magical, ineffable, intangible little

something. The ghost in the machine, the observer, the believer... the soul.

This is the season we celebrate the birth of a man whose ideas changed the world. That a life could be lived as a sacrifice - that Love – could be the embodiment of God and his followers could love, not just their neighbors... but their enemies.

Not an easy faith, sure, but it's a good one. And a reason to celebrate. Merry Christmas!

...MAYBE A DRINKING PROBLEM??

People do funny stuff when they're drunk. You know the stuff.

You find your phone full of photos with someone you don't know. Doing things you don't usually do... in ways you probably shouldn't do them... lots of sad, weird, things. But for most people – these are rare, funny, awkward memories and you shuffle off with a bit of shame, and a reminder that you don't want to do that again for a while.

But...

But, I get the feeling that there are some people for whom the funny stuff they do drunk is not just a once a year moment of shame. I get the feeling that it's a chronic issue that's affecting our lives with unforeseen consequences

Things I think we may need to blame on alcohol:

Daylight saving time. There's a purported saying by a Native American in reference to daylight savings. That only a white man would cut the bottom off of a blanket, sew it onto the top and claim to have made a bigger blanket. Good point.

That white man may have just been drunk. I can't think

of a good reason to put our lives through this nonsense. Honestly. We could just start school a half hour later all year long. Done. Businesses could just open a half hour later, or, if it seemed more prudent, have summer and winter hours. Easy peasy. I cannot tell you how many times Arizona's wisdom has been referenced in our home during the "spring forward week.

Another drunk people thing?? Early out Wednesday.

Honestly. I have never heard of this anywhere else on earth. Never.

And there's a reason. It's a terrible idea!

Who on earth likes this? I have lived in Montrose for 10 years and I have never ever once met anyone who liked the early out Wednesdays. Not one. Where are the defenders of this idea? If we are going to get out early one day I'd like to move for Fridays.

Or... follow me here... this might sound crazy... but how about we just have every school day last the exact same amount of time?? Take an extra week for summer break if you need. Win, win, win. I mean, if we want to be innovative – let's copy Garfield county and switch to four days a week!! Yay!!!

It just blows my mind that more than a decade ago there was a conversation where they said... "Let's make summer a week shorter, and instead we will make the entire town plan every Wednesday to have to pick up children and figure out childcare one hour longer on Wednesdays. I have a feeling that the folks in that meeting weren't sipping coffee... you know... you know?? Wink -wink.

Another drunk person idea? Road work during peak driving hours.

So – Californians have a sober minded logic to road work. They do it in the middle of the night. Californians are not a group that I have an insurmountable amount of respect for. (The mountable respect I have is beyond small. Like a child's stool.) They pay too much in taxes, blow all their money on empty public transit systems and they are not a tough bunch.

On a scale of toughness from 0-10 where 0 is a big, whiney, baby and 10 is Chuck Norris... Californians merit a 2... maybe. But they manage to handle using the graveyard shift for road work. It's brilliant – right? Work on the roads when almost no-one is driving on them. I mean, your nurses and doctors and gas station attendants are all capable of graveyard shifts.

But – if the solution is more taxes then forget it. (That's always the stinking answer when drunk people plan stuff.)

Other drunk people ideas:

The new leggings as pants look, early out Wednesdays (Yes, I'm saying it again. Honestly - this idea is just the worst... like bunkbed couches), skiing moguls, folding fitted sheets, trying anything you ever saw on Pinterest, politics these days – I mean...right?

Clearly drunk people are running far too much of our country. It appears to me that the "powers that be" are in need of a 12-step program. The first step is admitting you have a problem.

FIND YOUR SOLUTION...

Kneel down on the shore, be thirsty no more. Go under and be purified.

Water. It's nothing big.

Plain, tasteless, odorless, boring.

It just satiates us. Hydrates the fruit trees. The stuff of life, of survival, of cleansing, healing, cleaning. It's everything.

Water is no easy subject. It's too obvious, too straightforward. But, it's so profound in its complete, desperate necessity that we are moved to deeply mortal, foundational, and ultimately, spiritual things.

The earliest "gods" are discussed in the Enuma Elish. These writings are some of the very earliest writings ever discovered. The earliest faith practices on record ever. They discuss the vital gods of water. They are the birth of the faith of the people of Ur – the land of Canaan... a man would be born there who would change his name and create a tribe. Abraham.

Ea. God of the water... where fertility is born. God of life: where the water goes... things grow. God of intelligence, power and subtlety. It's passive in flowing, but nothing can stop it. Water is always moving, always headed back to where it has been. From the sky to the soil to the ocean to the sky. A powerful, unstoppable force... and yet completely effortless. Because of its powerless power the Taoists use it as an analogy. That religion believes conflict and discord are always caused by fighting nature. That peace and happiness are achieved only when you accept the flow and omnipotence of the universe, the ultimate expression of their belief is water. It's accomplishing everything, achieving all... and never struggling. It's simply is what it is.

A Mikvah is a Jewish holy bathing ritual. We rural middle Americans practice the art in our day as Baptism. Washing away the old, embracing the new. It's sacred. Holy water. The power to transform hearts, souls. You enter, you change.

Who of us hasn't had that day? Hot, sweaty, dusty, dry. And then... a shower? A river? A rainstorm? The salty, oily, dusty film that chokes us is met with the pure, clean water. We step into liquid. And there is just something there. We feel life. We were made for this.

When your head is submerged in water the unique 'mammalian diving reflex' changes your body in dramatic ways. Your blood pressure drops, your heart rate slows... often dramatically. We can hold our breath for dramatic times – believed impossible just a few years ago: 14-15 minutes. It may sound outlandish, but it's true. Humans can hold our breath for times such as these.

In Western Medicine just years ago, this was nonesense. But, in the diving communities of old Japanese matriarchs... this was well known. Because, what we had forgotten... what our hard, driving, entrepreneurial minds had lost, was a knowledge that we are a marine creature. Well suited to a life in the sea. We have forgotten the Polynesian roots we all have descended from. A people who once crossed the entire planet fearlessly. Because those who followed with books and writing never wrote those stories.

We need light, love, soil, air... and water. It's is 70% of our body mass. It is 70% of our planet. It needs no conservation for its existence... there is plenty. The abundance is clear... but, we pipe, move, conserve, fight, vote, pay, die for it... because our need is so desperate.

Whatever your problem – the solution is water. Tears, sweat, baptism, a swim. Go to the water. Find your cure. It's in there... somewhere.

A LOOK AT THAT PREGNANCY GLOW

How is sex at all fair? That is ALL that men contribute to the process? Have an orgasm? Seriously? I have to go through nine of the all time worst months of my entire life – and then the childbirth – and then the breastfeeding. His body's contribution? Sex. I kind of hate men for this.

About That Pregnancy Glow, the debut book by author Twyla Righter, is a laugh out loud journey through the joys and pains of pregnancy and early motherhood. It is a fun, crass, and heartfelt look at the greatest year of a woman's life. You'll laugh, you'll learn and you'll remember just why every bit of annoying, overwhelming, painful suffering is worth it.

AVAILABLE NOW ON AMAZON

ABOUT THE AUTHOR

For several years Twyla Righter has spent her time developing a specialized skill set. She can change a diaper on a squirming toddler – one handed. She can cook a dinner with an appropriate vegetable to carbohydrate/cheese ratio while quizzing a spelling test and refereeing a dramatic game of tag. She can teach a teenager to drive a manual and not completely lose her mind. These skills have yet to prove all that helpful to the world at large (but, the one handed diaper trick is a hit at parties.)

Twyla Righter lives in Colorado with a ridiculously sexy rock-climber and their three spawn.

www.ingramcontent.com/pod-product-compliance
Lightning Source LLC
LaVergne TN
LVHW041540070426
835507LV00011B/849